DEVILS
WILL REIGN

WILBUR S. SHEPPERSON SERIES

IN NEVADA HISTORY

The Unspiked Rail: Memoir of a Nevada Rebel

The Ignoble Conspiracy: Radicalism on Trial in Nevada
(with Guy Louis Rocha)

Jack Longstreet: Last of the Desert Frontiersmen

Goldfield: The Last Gold Rush on the Western Frontier

Ghost Dance Winter and Other Tales of the Frontier

*A Mine of Her Own: Women Prospectors in the
American West, 1850–1950*

Sarah Winnemucca

The Glory Days in Goldfield, Nevada

DEVILS
Will Reign

➤❘ **How Nevada Began** ❘◀

SALLY ZANJANI

▲▲ UNIVERSITY OF NEVADA PRESS

RENO & LAS VEGAS

Wilbur S. Shepperson Series in Nevada History
Series Editors: Michael Green

University of Nevada Press, Reno, Nevada 89557 USA
Copyright © 2006 by University of Nevada Press
Manufactured in the United States of America
Design by Omega Clay

Library of Congress Cataloging-in-Publication Data
Zanjani, Sally Springmeyer, 1937–
    Devils will reign : how Nevada began / by Sally Zanjani.
        p. cm. — (Wilbur S. Shepperson series in Nevada history)
    Includes bibliographical references and index.
    ISBN 0-87417-663-8 (hardcover : alk. paper)
1. Nevada—History. 2. Frontier and pioneer life—Nevada.
3. Nevada—Ethnic relations. I. Title. II. Series.
    F841.Z36 2006
    979.3—dc22   2005025896

The paper used in this book meets the requirements
of AmericanNational Standard for Information Sciences—
Permanence of Paper for Printed Library Materials,
ANSI Z.48-1984. Binding materials were selected
for strength and durability.

First Printing

15 14 13 12 11 10 09 08 07 06   5 4 3 2 1

*To the pioneer
grandparents I never knew,
Herman Henry and
Wilhelmine Springmeyer*

CONTENTS

ILLUSTRATIONS

MAPS

ACKNOWLEDGMENTS

I AM GRATEFUL TO Charles Wegman for allowing me full use of the Grosh Papers and to Fred Holabird for bringing us together. My debt to Eric Moody at the Nevada Historical Society for invaluable advice on sources cannot be overstated.

Other colleagues at libraries, historical societies, and museums provided much aid and many courtesies. Special mention should be made of Peter Blodgett, Huntington Library; Jody Cary, New York Historical Society; Lee Brumbaugh, Nevada Historical Society; Joyce Cox, Kathy Edwards, Jeff Kintop, Guy Louis Rocha, and Susan Searcy at the Nevada State Library and Archives; Ronald James, Nevada Historic Preservation Office; and Robert Nylen, Nevada State Museum. Lillis Hunter and Jane McMeans kindly shared their family histories with me; Benjamin Damonte gave generous assistance; and Stanley Paher provided useful comments.

Carolyn Garner at the Huntington Library and Marion Ellison in the Carson Valley gave helpful research assistance. Cartography was done by Paul Cirac.

DEVILS
WILL REIGN

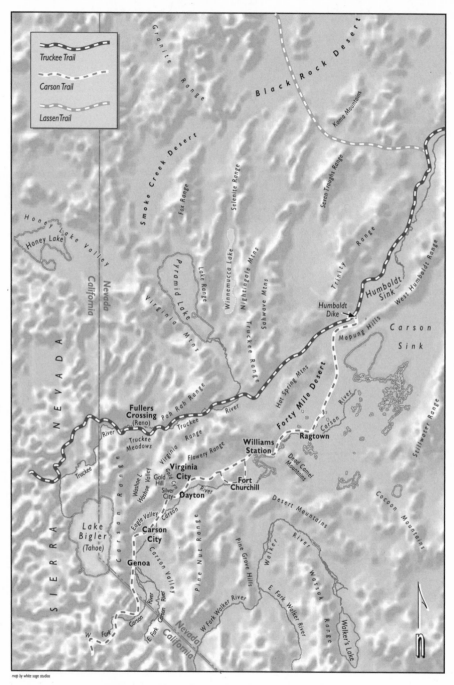

Settlements in Western Nevada Territory, 1861.

Where Three Worlds Met

I T WAS A TIME when mighty pines unbitten by the ax still stood tall in the Sierra Nevada, deer moved softly through the forest shade, rivers rippled in clear cascades down the eastern slope to flow more gently through valleys of deep grass and lose themselves in desert lakes and marshes, antelope still flicked their short white tails and bounded with springing leaps across sage-sprinkled hills quilted with tall bunches of Indian rice grass, and golden eagles soared above the mountain chains that crossed the desert, north to south, again and again, from the Sierra Nevada almost to the Great Salt Lake.

This pristine natural world, long undisturbed, was about to be shattered. After the discovery of gold in California in 1848, migration to the West, so tentatively begun, turned into a flood. More than twenty-two thousand crossed Nevada by the emigrant trails in 1849 and, in passing, stimulated the trading stations that became the first settlements. It was a time when emigrants, both fearful and contemptuous of the lurking Indians, tramped wearily beside their plodding oxen, passing through a long graveyard of dead beasts, discarded household heirlooms, and indispensable machines. This hot, barren desert and the mighty wall of mountains that guarded it in the West were the last and most terrible ordeal of a journey optimistically begun months earlier at the edge of the Plains. All was stripped to the essentials now—life, water, food, and somehow putting one foot ahead of the other.

Indians looked down from their mountain strongholds and saw covered wagons pulled by big, slow-moving beasts. The owl-faced, bearded white people who walked alongside had shown themselves unfriendly, and often dangerous, when Indians tried to approach, and obviously these newcomers understood little about finding water and food in a land not their own, and even less about sharing. As they selfishly kept their stock for themselves, it had been necessary to slip in by night and run off some of the stock that they failed to offer for roasting over the coals of a campfire. Still, these white men had made strange and marvelous inventions, and the Indians would have liked very much to try on their hats.

In Washington the 1840s and 1850s were a time when widening division over the issue of slavery in the territories was nearing a crisis point that could be settled only on the bloody killing fields of the Civil War. Compromises were carefully crafted in Congress, only to crumble. Certain presidents toyed with the sort of imperialist solutions more often associated with swashbuckling buccaneers. James Polk, for one, might well have annexed northern Mexico if Whigs in the opposing party had not blocked the plan, and he tried to buy Cuba. Washington politics would have more effect on the creation of Nevada than anything done in Nevada. All the same, the circumstance that the final decision on their future rested elsewhere did little to lessen the struggles of the contending parties on the front lines.

Remember that the outcomes were not foreordained—or, at least, they did not seem so to those who lived through them. With the benefit of hindsight, we may conclude that strong, fundamental forces produced inevitable results, but to the men of the 1850s, a broad range of possibilities—some of them quite mad to our eyes—seemed not merely visionary but likely. To study the early settlers, then, is not only to trace the lives they lived in this remote frontier outpost and the conflicts between them but also, and perhaps most important, to consider the variety and enormity of their ambitions. What Nevada did to them is a matter of record. What they expected of Nevada is the subtler issue that shades and defines their lives.

Nevada, of course, is a misnomer, used here as a convenience in place of lengthier, more cumbersome terms. In the 1850s, when the story begins, this large, empty space on the map had not yet attained a separate identity and a name. This is important because out of the formless chaos many things might be created. The very plasticity of the place extended the range of possibilities and fed the fires of ambition. Anything could happen—and did.

Because they left no record of their visions of the future, Indian hopes must be inferred from their circumstances as traditional hunter-gatherer peoples who had lived in much the same way for centuries. The Washo, who made their home on the eastern edge of the Sierra Nevada, in Carson Valley, Eagle Valley, Washoe Valley, and the Truckee Meadows, still followed the old mountain paths for summer fishing and camping at the Lake of the Sky (present Lake Tahoe). The Paiutes, who inhabited most of the rest of western Nevada, still gathered at Pyramid Lake for the annual fish run, at the Humboldt Sink for the mud-hen hunt, and in autumn made their way into the mountains where blue-green piñon trees grew to gather nuts. The Paiutes seem to have harbored no territorial ambitions, and no other Indian tribes contended with them for the harsh desert lands that barely sustained them. Minor shifts might have been foreseen, perhaps a raid for women on the Shoshone tribe to the east or a journey over the Sierra Nevada to trade with California Indian tribes. But these were incremental. Probably, Indian hopes extended no further than a good year, when the game would be plentiful, the nut harvest bountiful, and the storms of winter that made them shiver in their thin reed *kahnees* and brush shelters not too cruel.

In 1850 the great Paiute leaders that history remembers could already be distinguished: old Chief Truckee who extended the hand of friendship to the white men, guided the early emigrant parties on safe passages across the deserts and turned his people toward the path of peace; his son-in-law, Winnemucca, the shaman chief and wily diplomat who would attempt every device that ingenuity could devise to save his people and finally embark upon a philosophical quest to understand the catastrophe that struck them down; Numaga, the war chief who, when his pleas for peace had failed, inflicted the most decisive defeat that a settler army had suffered in years; and finally Sarah, daughter of Winnemucca, still a child in 1850 but one day to become the eloquent voice of the Paiutes who would interpret, lecture, write, and testify in the long battle to win justice for her people. Watching from afar while the "houses on wheels," as Sarah called the emigrant wagons, moved slowly across their deserts, none but Winnemucca in his shaman dreams could know that the good years were gone forever.

To the emigrants, the vision was California, the golden land, where they would make their fortunes in gold easily plucked from soft earth and gentle streams and return home as rich and important men to the accolades of family and friends. Or perhaps they might start new farms in rich, summery valleys where snow never fell, far from the frozen lands from which they came. If they were young men freed from office routine or farm drudgery and the strictures of respectability, it would be a grand adventure, a chance to cut loose, run wild, camp out with the boys, and do all the things they could never do at home. But first they must cross this fearful desert, these towering mountains, and put this miserable ordeal behind them.

Later, when the backwash from California began, some would return, hoping to re-create the excitement of early California on a newer frontier. They saw profit in the wagons of struggling emigrants in need of provisions and fresh animals; if there was gold in California, might these mountains also hold their share? Later still came settlers with higher ambitions than profit or finding another frontier. They saw a larger picture—Nevada as the springboard from which they would vault to high political office, perhaps in a new state, perhaps even in a new nation composed of the Far West.

[4]

The Mormons who made the journey also followed a trajectory of increasing ambition. The first to arrive envisaged only a way station to reap profit from the emigrant trade, and in the 1850s the Mormons established several such way stations in Wyoming and Nebraska, where they raised hay and sold supplies to travelers and sometimes ran a ferry. The larger vision, however, was that of the Church of Jesus Christ of Latter-day Saints president, Brigham Young, and he was nothing if not a man of vision. He saw the eastern slope of the Sierra Nevada as a gathering place where arriving converts would collect prior to making the journey across the desert to Utah, where their numbers would strengthen the theocratic community he was building. In this utopia Mormons would be so overwhelmingly dominant that they could freely practice their faith without fear of the persecutions that had destroyed their communities in Missouri and Illinois. Because not even the Mormons proved capable of founding a successful settlement in Las Vegas, Nevada's swift evolution from terra incognita to territory would be played out in the settlements on the eastern slope of the Sierra Nevada. In time, events suggest that the Mormon colony in northern Nevada began to assume a larger role as the anchor on the western periphery of a Mormon inland empire and future state.

The position of the eastern slope as the periphery appears central to the ensuing events. On the periphery, where the worlds of Indians, frontiersmen, and Mormons met, conflict may well have been inevitable.

The First Settlers Arrive, 1851

ABNER BLACKBURN was a Mormon, after a fashion. Born in Pennsylvania in 1827, third child in a westering family that moved to Ohio, then joined the Church of Jesus Christ of Latter-day Saints in Missouri and Nauvoo, Illinois, he was not baptized until 1847, later than other members of his family. Moreover, he entertained certain reservations about the church from an early point. As a teenager at the Nauvoo colony, he remembered: "About this time I began to weaken on the whole outfit and thought the Saints were no better than the Gentiles were. Concequently I quit and went steamboating." Nonetheless, he served in the Mexican American War with the Mormon Battalion, then accompanied Brigham Young's wagon train heading westward in 1847 as a teamster. Soon afterward he joined a Mormon party headed for California. Even allowing for the fact that by the time he began his memoirs in 1889 he had turned into a full-blown skeptic, his humor at the expense of the pious Captain James Brown displays an unmistakable lack of reverence: "We broke in on his devotions [and] cried out 'Supper!' and had a good laugh on him the rest of the trip."[1]

More than he was a Mormon, Blackburn was a frontiersman, "fond of excitement and adventure, always wishing to go West." If the wiry youth with unruly black hair and an unflinching gaze had not already earned the title when steamboating on the upper Missouri and trekking westward with Young, he certainly did so in 1847 when Young sent him to California in a party headed by Captain James Brown to collect payments owed to the Mormon Battalion for their service in the Mexican American War and bring mail to church members in California. At that time the passage across the Great Basin remained little known and much feared. Only fourteen years had passed since the mountain man Joseph Reddeford Walker crossed in 1833, massacred a number of Paiutes, and established the route as an emigrant trail. In 1841 the Bartleson-Bidwell party became the first emigrants to cross, guided in the last stage by nothing more than a vague belief that California lay to the west and unable to later explain exactly where they had blundered across the Sierra Nevada. Just three years later John Charles Frémont ranged through, disparaging the land before him ("The rocks are volcanic, and the hills here have a burnt appearance—cinders and coals occasionally appearing as at a blacksmith's forge") but by his widely publicized writings shifting it from a terra incognita to a place on the map where travelers would at least know what to expect, albeit little that was good. Later in the same year the Stevens party, shown the way by Paiute chief Truckee, became the first to cross the Sierra Nevada with wagons. The year of Blackburn's journey, 1847, was also the year that the last of the Donner party finally left their "cannibal camp" in the Sierra Nevada. There Blackburn a few months later "stood guard in the latter part of the night and thought of all the ghosts and hobgoblins I could think of or ever heard of. Besides the sculls, bones, and the dark forrest, it was a most dismal place."[2]

Blackburn underwent considerable hardship on the Brown party's October return from California, which he called "the biggest torn fool erant that ever is known." Driving a herd of half-wild horses and menaced by Indians, the men hungered: "There was an awful goneness in our stomacks all the time. One of our messmates . . . would take the hare skins and scorch the fur off over the fire and then rost them to a turn. He sayed they went splendid." They lost the faint trail they had been following and ate snow with the horses after their water ran out. Blackburn came to believe that the desert was no place for man: "He

[7]

was out of his lattitude or his natural seane." When they finally neared the Salt Lake Valley, Captain Brown cried out in relief, "Toot your horn, Gabriel! We are most there."[3]

Of course, Blackburn returned as soon as he could, joining a pack train headed for the California gold country in the spring of 1849. Although another candidate for the distinction has been suggested, Blackburn may have been the first to discover mineral in Gold Canyon. While the party rested their animals by the Carson River, Blackburn wondered why there should not also be gold on the eastern side of the Sierra Nevada:

> The next day, while they were playing cards, I took a bread pan and a butcher knife and went out in the raveins to prospect and found gold in small quantities in three places. Went to a larger raveine and whear the watter run down over the bed rock a little on the side of the gulch. Dug down in the slate and found a fair prospect and kept paning for an hour or more. Went to camp and all hand[s] grabed up pans, knives, and kettles and started out. We scrached, scraped, and paned until nearly sun down and took out nine or ten dollars worth of gold. Being without tools and nearly out of provisions, we were compeld to abandon the place, but calculated to return some time in the future.[4]

His next trip, led by Captain Joseph DeMont in the spring of 1850, would prove momentous for the settlement of Nevada. The eighty-person party was a large one because, in Blackburn's words: "It was not much work to find men to goe to the new Eldorado. In those times, California was the only magnet." According to Hampton S. Beatie, another member of the party, they intended to mine briefly and then return to Salt Lake City. Blackburn, now a seasoned frontiersman of twenty-three, had never been enthusiastic about the desert scenery ("The mountains looked like they had been burnt with some great heat. The rocks would ring like crockery ware, with no timber in sight, only willows on the river. The alkily covered the plains"), and his observations on the journey sound distinctly blasé: "There was the

Frontiersman Abner Blackburn, about 1867. Courtesy
Special Collections, J. Willard Marriott Library, University of
Utah, Salt Lake City.

usual amount of wild Indians and the same shage brush, alkily, and
one range after another of low mountains and it was verry monotinous
to the view."[5]

Although the scenery and the Indians were much as he remembered, the 1849 gold rush had wrought a tremendous change. "The
emegrants began to overtake us and said thousands and thousands
were on the road comeing in every way." This news led to a sudden
change in plans: instead of mining the goldfields, the DeMont party
would mine the emigrants. Blackburn, the man "best acuainted with

the country," chose the site of Mormon Station (present Genoa) in the Carson Valley for a trading station.[6]

The site held promise because the meadows of the Carson Valley offered an oasis of recovery for travelers exhausted by their journey across the desert. Also, it was well positioned near the Carson Trail, the work of a party from the Mormon Battalion returning to Utah from California in 1848 and for a while the most popular passage across the Sierra Nevada, and the Georgetown Cutoff (joining Johnson Pass, roughly the route of present Highway 50). Blackburn's party built a corral for stock and a twenty-by-sixty-foot cabin with two rooms and no roof or floor, the first permanent structure in Nevada and the basis for Genoa's proud claim to be Nevada's first town because although other floating trading stations operating from tents appeared along the emigrant trail, none boasted anything so substantial as a roofless cabin and a corral. At Mormon Station, one emigrant observed an early example of the tinge of unorthodoxy that often infected Nevada Mormons: "They were playing cards & drinking liquor in fine stile."[7]

Business was brisk from the start. Blackburn, Beatie, and companions took several teams to Sacramento for supplies, packing the wagons on the way with Sierra Nevada snow, valuable in the heat and humidity of Sacramento. After their return to the Carson Valley, they sold the provisions for prices that led one emigrant to call their operation "a perfect skinning post." They also traded in stock, buying from travelers wasted animals for slaughter or subsequent resale, after grazing in the meadows had restored their strength, and selling good horses and mules for the difficult haul over the summit that emigrants called "the elephant's back." "On the whole we done very well down there," observed Beatie.[8]

They might have done even better. Blackburn scratched around Gold Canyon for a week or so, then gave it up, noting that other miners had been working there since his exploration of the previous year: "If we had known [of] the rich mines higher up the canion, the outcome would be different. We mist the great Bonanza and we come back to the station." In his poverty-stricken old age, it was an incident to be ruefully recalled. But, in truth, Abner Blackburn lacked the temperament of a miner. Not for him to burrow molelike in the earth for months and years in hope of treasure. New adventure was his gold. In future years he would battle with the Indians, settle in California among dissident Mormons, marry (in its way a new adventure) and father a large brood, and embark upon a whaling ship to the South Seas to sow "my wild oats" as a leave of absence from domesticity, but he made just one more journey across the Great Basin. Now that the trail, once so faint that he and his companions lost it, had been beaten into a virtual highway forty feet wide by thousands of emigrant wagons, the desert passage had become too easy.[9]

Already in 1850 scratching around Gold Canyon had developed into a minor rush. Emigrants reported meeting several trains a day headed for the site and "gold hunters ranging over the mountains." Nonetheless, these prospectors, like Blackburn, missed the great bonanza and found too little to justify remaining when the weather turned colder. Only James Finney ("Old Virginny"), who later took part in the discovery at Gold Hill that presaged the 1859 rush to the Comstock and saw Virginia City named in his honor, stayed through the winter, mostly in an alcoholic stupor, holed up in an earthen dugout in the mountainside. No others shared his persistence or his whiskey. In many ways, Finney was the quintessential Nevadan. Rumor had it that he had earlier mined in Volcano, California, changed his name from Fennimore to Finney after murdering a man, and moved on to Gold Canyon. It seems fitting that this tough reprobate of a prospector, undeterred by hardship and complete isolation, living on whiskey and hope, is now recognized as Nevada's first permanent settler. He would die two years after the rush began, thrown from a bucking horse when "bully drunk."[10]

Travelers saw the Carson Valley trading station as an oasis of civilization, not only for its meadows, its pure waters, and its solid structures but also for its families, with "handsome well dressed women"

Tentatively identified as James "Old Virginny" Finney
when young. Courtesy Nevada Historical Society, Reno.

and "prattling children." But civilization had not yet come to stay. At
the end of the travel season, the party sold their station to a Stockton
trader named Moore and packed up, lock, stock, and barrel—handsome women, prattling children, and all—and headed back to Salt
Lake City. It was there, while clerking in a store owned by the Reeses,
that Beatie talked about the Carson Valley venture and no doubt mentioned that they had done very well.[11]

This gave Colonel John Reese an idea. In the spring he set out on a
two-month journey with about thirteen wagons carrying plows, eggs,
bacon, flour, "seeds of all kinds," and other provisions. He arrived in
early June 1851, close to the site of the original trading station, which
he eventually bought from Moore. He would have noted a quarter section of land staked off a couple of weeks earlier by George Chorpen-

ning, supervisor of the first U.S. mail run between Sacramento and
Salt Lake. Another settler, J. R. "Poker" Brown, had arrived from Salt
Lake City earlier than Reese in May when no other white man lived
in the valley, claimed land, and planted a small potato patch. But
Chorpenning was generally absent on his mail runs, and Poker Brown,
really more prospector than rancher, divided his time between Gold
Canyon and the Carson Valley. Consequently, although Reese had not
been "first on the ground," as the saying went, there is justification for
the place of "first Carson Valley settler" that has usually been accorded
to him because he did, at least, stay settled. Others set up trading stations on the western portion of the emigrant trail and departed when
the travel season ended, but Reese differed from most in that he "put
in ground," presently selling his turnips for prices that amazed him,
and embarked upon an ambitious building program at the site already
known as Mormon Station in California newspapers, travel accounts,
and a guidebook. His seventeen-man crew built a two-story combination hotel and store and a number of cabins and fenced thirty acres.
Due to reports of cholera and Indian hostilities, emigration dropped
sharply in 1851. Nonetheless, Reese expected a better year to come and
counted upon supplying the miners he anticipated would be irre-
sistibly drawn back to Gold Canyon. He was not disappointed. Some
120 prospectors ranged over the mountains that year, and the estimated gold production of sixty thousand dollars suggests considerable
activity.[12]

"Eighteen fifty-two was a splendid year," said Reese. "Enough could
not be raised to supply the demand." He added a blacksmith shop and
planted grains and melons, as well as those lucrative turnips. Emigration resumed full steam, and miners continued to scratch the hills.
Permanent settlers began to arrive, including blacksmith Henry Van
Sickle, later known primarily for killing the desperado Sam Brown.[13]

Not all the newcomers were upstanding citizens. Van Sickle related
that Reese's fortifications against thieves were needed because "whites
were in some instances as bad as the red skins." Although Reese men-

tions the arrival of John Redden in Jack's Valley about three miles
north of Mormon Station, he does not indicate that he knew Redden
engaged in business other than ranching. Thefts of stock by Indians
along the trail occurred frequently, and the emigrants observed suspiciously that some of the supposed Indians spoke good English. The
belief gained credence that Mormons led these Indian predators in
robbery and murder. Major Jacob H. Holeman, Indian agent in Salt
Lake City, wrote to the commissioner of Indian affairs: "The *white* Indians, I apprehend, are much more dangerous than the *red*. The rene-
gades, deserters and thieves, who have had to fly from justice in California, have taken refuge in the mountains, and having associated
themselves with the Indians are more savage than the Indians themselves. By their cruelty to the whites, they have stimulated the Indians
to acts of barbarity, which they were never known to be guilty of before." Holeman also reported that a Mormon driving a cattle herd west
from Utah received quiet advice to paint the horns of his cattle so that
the thieves he encountered would see that his herd was not to be molested because it belonged to one of the brethren.[14]

The Reddens differ from others whom historian Dale L. Morgan
has called "murderous presences of the night" only in that Morgan
succeeded in uncovering their criminal history all the way back to
Devil Creek, across the river from the Mormon community of Nauvoo,
Illinois. Headed by old George Grant, the Reddens were an outlaw
family reminiscent of classic western films such as *Man of the West*
and nominally Mormon. At least, they made the trek west from Illinois with Brigham Young before applying their talents to the many
opportunities for plunder on the emigrant trails. Jack, connected by
marriage to other crime families on a par with his own, may have been
the Mormon referred to in agent Holeman's letter who belonged "to a
company of white men and Indians who are stationed near the Carson
Valley" with the aim of robbing the emigrants. It may have been he
who tendered advice on painting cattle horns. He underwent a temporary inconvenience when jailed in Salt Lake City for horse theft in

1854, but nothing to seriously cramp his style. Redden and the other murderous presences of the night cast a shadow over the future. Many Gentiles feared and distrusted the Mormons and their Indian allies; many Mormons slept with guns handy in fear of frontier roughs drifting in with the backwash from California.[15] And time would show these fears were well founded on both sides.

In a period when few blacks participated in the western migration, a group of successful black pioneers in the Carson Valley merits special mention. In 1853 Ben Palmer and David Barber, a white man married to Palmer's sister Charlotte, took out land claims on the west side of the valley about five miles south of Genoa, where another black family, the Millers, soon joined them on a neighboring ranch. Ben Palmer persisted and prospered. Despite his illiteracy, by 1875 he became the tenth-largest taxpayer in the valley, with a large cattle herd and many fine horses. He also kept a pack of hounds, which could be heard baying in the mountains at night when Palmer went hunting. His sister Charlotte became known for her hospitality and her curiosity. One old settler recalled: "Come by anywhere near noon, you didn't get by. You had to stop and have dinner and they'd find out everything you knew." The store of information she acquired may have contributed to Charlotte's reputation as a prophetess. As political scientist Elmer Rusco observes, during an era of legal discrimination against Nevada blacks, when they were later barred from voting, attending public schools, and marrying whites, the success of these black pioneers and the respect they enjoyed from their neighbors are "remarkable." At Charlotte Barber's funeral in 1887, the local newspaper reported: "The procession was one of the largest ever witnessed in Douglas County."[16]

Another memorable early arrival was William B. Thorington. He was neither a Mormon (although his marital practices might have led to some confusion) nor a thief (although those who gambled with him might have disputed it). Above all, he possessed that quality easiest to recognize in life and most difficult to capture in print—charisma. "In form he was large, weighing 200 pounds, and with broad, ample shoulders, stood six feet and one inch in height; his head, covered with glossy curling hair colored like the raven's wing, was massive, with a high classic forehead, and large gray mirthful eyes, looking out from beneath projecting eyebrows, that indicated strong perceptive faculties. The country had no handsomer or merrier citizen in it."[17]

Born in Chenango County in western New York in 1812, he married Maria, a striking beauty with black hair and great brown eyes. The couple had one son, Jerome, born about 1842. In 1848 the Thoringtons began heading west as a family—Bill, his wife and child, and his parents. They first landed in Michigan, then joined the California gold rush, perhaps as early as 1848. "This was the rendezvous of the thieves and gamblers who came out from California to fleece the emigrants," observed G. W. Thissell, who watched Bill gambling in August 1849 at a trading station about twelve miles northwest of present-day Fallon, known as Ragtown for the tattered clothes the emigrants hung on the bushes to dry after washing them in the Carson River. The possibility also arises that Bill was himself a forty-niner pausing to take advantage of the opportunities that Ragtown presented. The certainty is that Bill always emerged from these games the winner. Thissell's friend lost his only ox, plus all his money and everything he could borrow, and had to beg his way to California. Bill had already acquired a profession well suited to the times but apparently new to him and gained the sobriquet that, in the end, would seem ironic: he became the gambler "Lucky Bill."[18]

The American public in the nineteenth century already may have been well acquainted with Lucky Bill without knowing it because he reportedly was the model for the gambler Jack Hamlin in Bret Harte's popular gold rush stories. So far as appearances go, the similarity seems slight because the warm, extroverted Lucky Bill shows little of the cool, restrained style, the "Homeric gravity," or the "smile of cynical philosophy" characteristic of Hamlin. Yet some of Hamlin's qualities do appear reminiscent of Lucky Bill—his relations with women, for one. The writer of an 1855 article on Lucky Bill observed only half jokingly: "It is said he contemplates joining the Mormons, and taking to his heart twenty or thirty wives. . . . The next we shall hear of him will probably be as a Mormon prophet, with fifty wives and concubines."[19]

Lucky Bill's almost legendary gallantry, for another. Nevada's first historian, Myron Angel, recounts an incident recalled by early settlers—and it is but one of many:

> In 1854 a couple of California bound emigrants stopped at Mormon Station, and had a falling out, and it transpired that they were partners, one of them owning the wagon and cattle that hauled it, while the other, who had a wife, supplied the provisions. The expense . . . had exhausted the husband's finances, and the owner of the train refused to take the bankrupt emigrants any further. Lucky Bill passing, saw the woman weeping disconsolately by the wagon, and his sympathies were at once aroused. Upon inquiry he learned the state of affairs, and told the husband and wife . . . he would see that they reached Sacramento without delay. That night the owner of the outfit was induced to bet against Lucky Bill in his "thimble rig game," and in the morning he had neither an outfit nor a dollar in money left. The winner gave him back fifteen dollars of the money, bought him a new pair of boots to travel in, told him to "lite out" for California on foot, and never after that to bet against any one who was playing his own game. To the bankrupt family he gave a cow, spent the loser's money in buying them provisions, etc. and then hired a man to drive the team with them to California.

Generosity to old friends and destitute travelers often distinguished Lucky Bill. Although the evidence is less clear, Lucky Bill may have possessed a fine singing voice that also echoed in Jack Hamlin. It may not be too much to suggest that the popular image of the frontier gambler that took shape in the nineteenth century based upon Bret Harte's stories originated with Lucky Bill.[20]

At Sacramento in 1850, Lucky Bill quickly became a wealthy man by dealing monte and enticing the unwary to try their hands at the thimble-rigging game. One old acquaintance remembered seeing him

at all hours squatting in front of a gambling house, "artistically moving" three cups around, and offering to take bets. In 1851 he reportedly
made twenty-four thousand dollars in just two months.

> Bill's usual method of attracting custom was the cry of "Here, gentle-
> men, is a nice quiet little game conducted on the square, and especially
> recommended by the clergy for its honesty and wholesome moral ten-
> dencies. I win only from blind men; all that have two good eyes can win
> a fortune. You see, gentlemen, here are three little wooden cups, and
> here is a little ball, which, for the sake of starting the game, I shall place
> under this one, as you can plainly see; and now I shall place it under
> this one, as you can plainly see, and now I shall place it under this, the
> middle one, merely to show how much quicker the hand is than the eye,
> and removing it from the middle, quietly cover it with the other, thus—
> and thus—and thus; and now I will bet two, four, or six ounces that no
> gentleman can the first time trying, raise the cup that the ball is under;
> if he can, he can win all the money that Bill, by patient toil and industry,
> has scraped together."[21]

When the California legislature began to frown on gambling, Sacramento's gamblers shifted their operations to the gold rush camps in
the Sierra Nevada. Lucky Bill landed in Placerville but only briefly.
A mob ran him out of town after his brand of patient toil and industry
won fifteen hundred dollars from a prominent local citizen. Finding
themselves seated side by side on the stage the next morning, the
brother of Lucky Bill's victim drew his bowie knife, and Lucky Bill un-
limbered his Colt .36. Upon their request, the stage driver reined in
his horses so that the two could step out and settle their differences.
Although the knife flew through the air and the Colt blasted, no serious damage to either party resulted.[22]

A change of scene now seemed a wise move for Lucky Bill. He already knew the Carson Valley from his passage through it on his way
to California. He may have been accompanied by a close friend and
ally in dangerous times, William P. "Uncle Billy" Rogers. Known for

his ability to develop close ties with Indians, Uncle Billy had acted as liaison with the Indians who joined Frémont's forces during the short-lived and ineffectual Bear Flag revolt against Mexican rule of California in 1846. He later served as sheriff of El Dorado County, a jurisdiction including Placerville. Rogers, whose apparent preference for wilder, less crowded country suggests that California had grown too tame for him, probably had already headed for the Carson Valley.[23]

The Carson Valley held much promise for the likes of Lucky Bill. The passing emigrants meant lucrative business for a wealthy man with cash to invest in a toll road, a hotel, and other enterprises, and many of these travelers might be enticed to indulge in an occasional wager on the thimbles. Although Gold Canyon's population of one prospector in a burrow had expanded to perhaps 130 miners in 1852 and a party of men had built a station in Eagle Valley (present Carson City), the scattering of settlers in the valleys of the eastern slope remained sparse enough that opportunities abounded. And best of all, there were no officious busybodies to enact laws forbidding those little games of chance recommended by the clergy for honesty and moral tendencies. Indeed, there was only a rudimentary squatter government. It seemed like Lucky Bill's kind of place. He may have arrived as early as 1852 and certainly no later than 1853.[24]

Government, such as it was, had commenced on the eastern slope on November 12, 1851, when a small group of Mormon and Gentile settlers estimated at thirty to forty-five gathered at Mormon Station, adopted several measures to settle land claims, elected a seven-member governing committee that would, in turn, appoint a recorder and treasurer, and decided to petition Congress to make the region a "distinct Territorial Government" separate from Utah Territory—the first attempt by this motley crew to shape their own political future. Rule by Utah had scarcely been onerous, because Utah had as yet made no move to govern the area. Little more than a year had passed since September 9, 1850, when Congress granted statehood to California and created Utah Territory with the Great Basin and the eastern slope inside its boundaries, but already protest was brewing. The non-Mormon settlers anticipated the worst, as is shown in a letter from Lorenzo Dow to President Millard Fillmore and a December petition from this group to Congress. The petitioners protested their unwillingness to live under a theocracy that denied legal justice to "patriotic citizens of the Union" and their opposition to Mormon polygamy. They closed by threatening that if the constitutional rights they sought by peaceful means were denied, "we shall maintain them as our fathers did."[25]

In two additional meetings that November, the settlers adopted more measures governing land claims and declared timber to be common property. They also elected a magistrate, court clerk, and sheriff and declared that their elected officials would collectively constitute a court with sweeping powers to "*adjudicate summarily* in all cases of controversy." The traditional American fear of despotism tempered the court's authority, however. Should the court abuse its power, a court of inquiry consisting of twelve citizens "summoned promiscuously" would serve as a final court of appeal with the right to impose penalties upon the magistrate "in the event of abusive exercise of his authority."[26]

No such abuses occurred. Indeed, the newly elected officials proved inactive to the point of invisibility. If quarrels developed, nothing prevented them from taking an ugly turn. Blackburn recalled sprees at the trading station in which the boys would "cut up harness, bend guns around trees, run a lot of waggons togeather set them on fire and run amuck generly." This may have been harmless enough, but Blackburn noted ominously, "There was no law or gospel to hinder them."[27]

Indians, Emigrants, and Grand Ideas

I T WAS THE FAULT of the wind, that mischievous creature. After the Maker of All Things laid out the seeds that would become the Indian peoples in a flat basket, the wind blew away most of the Washo seeds, leaving only a few. In consequence, the Washo were a small tribe of fewer than a thousand clustered in the valleys of the eastern slope. Not only was the tribe small but also distinct from their neighbors the Paiutes, probably more than four times as numerous and ranging over a vast territory of thousands of miles to the north, the south, and the east; the Shoshone, still farther east; and the Southern Paiutes, a long distance to the southeast. All these eastern tribes spoke Uto-Aztecan languages, while Washo belonged to the ancient Hokan language group. Like the frontiersmen and the Mormons, the Washo also hovered on their own periphery, far removed from other Hokan-speaking tribes in northern and southern California, the central coast, and farther still in Mexico and Central America.[1]

Washo lands shaded into Paiute country east of the valleys in the mountain ranges, the Pine Nut and the Virginia. The Paiutes occupied the Pyramid Lake region and a portion of the Honey Lake Valley, the most northerly point of Washo territory. Although the two tribes had little liking for each other and occasionally skirmished, their relations never deteriorated into full-scale warfare because the struggle for survival in the austere conditions of the Great Basin preoccupied both of them. Some years later, when grouping the Washo and the Paiute in the same reservation was proposed, Nevada territorial governor James W. Nye rejected the idea on the ground that the tribes would engage in "incessant broil."[2] In this, he made no mistake.

By the harsh standards of the Great Basin, the Washo lived rather well. In summer they climbed the Sierra Nevada to fish in the waters of the sublimely beautiful Lake Tahoe. In fall they gathered acorns on the western slope and piñon nuts in the mountains to the east of their valleys. They hunted, fished the streams and rivers with ingenious weirs (enclosures for catching fish), and gathered seeds and other plant foods from the lush natural valley meadows. They wintered in the valleys, but when occasion demanded, they put on their snowshoes and skimmed like birds over the mountain snows. Their lives as hunter-gatherers necessitated a good deal of walking, for the Washo did not acquire the horse until very late. When a Washo girl became a woman and stood almost naked before the rising sun with her face and body marked with red ocher, her people offered a prayer for the most valuable asset a woman could possess: "Be light on your feet and walk long."[3]

Early contacts between Indians and emigrants on the California trails were not entirely negative. Watching the emigrants emerge from their covered wagons, the Washo thought the wagons gave birth to these alien creatures and later visited emigrant camps in a friendly way to satisfy their curiosity. Although emigrants initially viewed the Indians with a mixture of fear and contempt for their primitive way of life and rejected the cordial overtures of the Paiute chief Truckee, the early travelers soon accepted his help gladly and he became a famous emigrant guide. He used all his eloquent powers of persuasion to turn his people along the path of peace and friendship with his "white brothers," an imperfect peace, to be sure, but one that lasted for years to come.[4]

Mariett Cummings, an 1852 emigrant, thought the Paiutes friendly and intelligent and appreciated the small fish and berries they gave her. The following year another woman traveler wrote of her delight with the mink and other furs she received from the Indians in trade and her plan for a "pretty muff" to be made from the wildcat pelt they presented to her. While their exotic garb amused her ("He has had his hair cut & looks quite civilized having on a red flannel shirt & his legs covered with the sleeves of another the other Indian is dressed in skins & lots of ornaments"), she related that her emigrant company tried to persuade these two to accompany them as insurance against Indian hostilities.[5]

Hostilities with the Indians became increasingly likely as the massive influx of emigrants depleted Indian food supplies and the Indians began stealing stock. The Washo first met the cow when one strayed from a wagon train. They examined the exotic creature with puzzled interest, tried packing it, experimented with riding it, and finally killed and ate it. They quickly learned how to get more. Thefts by the Washo and the Paiutes of cattle, oxen, horses, and mules from the wagon trains multiplied, often by the method of shooting arrows at night to wound a few animals, which would then have to be abandoned by the emigrants. Large wagon trains well supplied with stock could afford the loss, but the thefts seriously hampered emigrants obliged to abandon their wagons and walk after the loss of their draft animals. From the time they set out on the eastern edge of the Plains, fear of Indians had loomed large in emigrant minds, although more would die from drowning, disease, and hardship than from Indian attacks. As a result, relatively few Indian incidents sufficed to intensify this deeply held fear to fury. One traveler noted: "The man to whom the two injured oxen belonged was in a rage of madness over his loss and insisted on all of the men shouldering their guns and hunting down these red skins: but the foolishness of such a move was soon made apparent to him."[6]

Cooler heads did not always prevail. A turning point arrived in early October 1850, when a large body of sixty Mormons driving four hundred horses and mules to Salt Lake City lost thirty head of stock to Indians. They vengefully killed and scalped six Washo, and rumor had it that a party of Missourians had already killed eighteen. From that year onward, the Washo no longer visited emigrant camps in a friendly way, and the name they gave to the white man, *mushege,* meant wild, fierce, and unpredictable, with overtones of insanity. Anticipating trouble with the Washo, the California governor ordered El Dorado County sheriff Rogers to raise a party of two hundred men to protect the emigrants in late October. Although Rogers complied, by then the travel season had practically ended. The sheriff mounted another effort in 1851, the Second El Dorado Expedition, which patrolled the trail from Ragtown through the Carson Valley. Authorities then chose to declare the Washo subdued, but the Washo thought otherwise. In 1852 Washo arrows flew toward the wagon trains from ambush in the willows along the banks of the Carson River. When bedded down for the night, an emigrant party heard what they mistook for the whistling wings of birds flying over their heads: "Day was breaking . . . when to our surprise and horror we found arrows all over the camp." Several cattle had been killed, but the emigrants fortunately escaped injury.[7]

In 1853 stock thefts finally reached the point at which some Carson Valley settlers pulled up stakes and left, and the rest determined to stop the Indians once and for all—and did. The next time the Indians swept down on the Genoa settlement, a party of forty or fifty angry pioneers armed with rifles rode out in pursuit. The Indians headed to the south end of the valley, then veered northeast toward the Pine Nut Mountains. They paused and fought in Long Valley. A number of Indians died before the battle shifted over the rocky lap of the hills to Horseshoe Bend. At this point, winding its way northward through canyons of piñons beneath lofty stone precipices, the East Carson River curves smoothly around a little valley cupped by gentler hills. Again they fought. More Indians died, and the survivors fled into the mountains, abandoning the stolen livestock by the riverbanks.[8]

For the Paiutes, worsening relations with the white invaders would one day end in war, and their shaman chief Winnemucca had already foreseen in a dream the future that lay before them:

[24]

I dreamt this thing three nights,—the very same. I saw the greatest emigration that has yet been through our country. I looked North and South and East and West, and saw nothing but dust, and I heard a great weeping. I saw women crying, and I also saw my men shot down by the white people. They were killing my people with something that made a great noise like thunder and lightning, and I saw the blood streaming from the mouths of my men that lay all around me. I saw it as if it was real.[9]

Despite this dark and prophetic vision, the Paiutes were more engaged with the white man as either aggressors or friends than the Washo. They adopted the horse (unlike the Washo) and committed more raids on the emigrants and their stock, yet at the same time they guided emigrants and traded with them, and they had strong leaders, old Truckee and his son-in-law Winnemucca, who were deeply committed to peace, no matter what provocations occurred, and wanted their people to learn the white man's ways. The Washo, lacking strong leaders, responded in a more diffuse way. Some clustered around white settlements and scavenged; others worked on the settlers' ranches; many withdrew. Ethnologist James Downs has aptly described their attitude toward whites as "one of avoidance and repressed hostility."[10]

Just how completely some Washo withdrew is illustrated by the experience of Herman and Wilhelmine Springmeyer (my grandparents) when they set up housekeeping in a cabin on their pioneer ranch in the Carson Valley in 1871. The Washo would gather at the windows to laugh and point at my grandmother as though the spectacle of a young German emigrant housewife going about her daily chores was a hilarious novelty—and this twenty years after the first settlers arrived in the Carson Valley.

Much that happened to the Washo in those years was far from amusing. In their myths they told of monsters, such as the whimpering giant Hanawiywiy and Ololing, the eyeless people-eating giant, but the effects of their sufferings from the settlers who made them beggars in their own land would be far worse than anything they had imagined at the hands of these fabled ogres. The old stories told of a clever, heroic woman, Nentusu, who was a powerful shaman. In the beginning, she commanded the storms to moisten the land, the piñon trees to grow, and the jackrabbits, the deer, and all the other animals to come to life so that her people might eat them. But in sorrow, after the killing of one of her children, she turned herself into a duck and flew away. Even in this time of need, she did not return.[11]

Who were these emigrant travelers whose passing brought the first traders and settlers to the eastern slope of an almost unknown region and disrupted the ancient way of life of the Indian peoples? Thousands, predominantly young men, passed over the California trails at the height of the gold rush in 1849. Relatively few were women. One traveler wrote that he could not help staring when he saw such a "novelty" and added: "Women seem to undergo the hardships of this journey with uncommon philosophy." In fact, many women may have been less philosophical than they seemed. Sarah Royce, mother of the famous California literary figure Josiah Royce, later wrote: "However brave a face I might have put on most of the time, I knew my coward heart was yearning all the while for a home nest."[12]

The emigrants started from east of the Great Plains in the spring as soon as the grasses that must feed their animals began to green and, recalling the horrible and well-known fate of the Donner party, worried that they might not make it across the Sierra Nevada before the snows fell. They came by a variety of conveyances, usually by ox-drawn, canvas-topped light wagons and more rarely by the large Conestogas of the gold rush image. Many packed their possessions on mules or horses, the disadvantage being that the packing must be done anew each morning. The packers could, of course, advance much more rapidly than the lumbering ox teams with their owners walking beside them at a rate of only fifteen miles a day or less. A surprisingly large number walked with their possessions on their backs. "Hundreds of men are footing it without team or provision," noted one diarist. A remarkable black woman carried a cast-iron baking oven on her head with her provisions and blanket piled on top. While other emigrants scorned them as tramps (probably often true) and "churlish, querulous fellows, who cannot well agree with associates," the walkers could cover nearly forty miles in a day and pity those encumbered with slow-moving teams. But they rarely knew where the next meal was coming from, for it must be begged, bought, or hunted.[13]

The great migration crossed the eastern slope and the Sierra Nevada by several trails. In early 1849 the most popular was the Carson, developed by Mormons returning from California in 1848. This trail proceeded from the Carson Valley through the cascade of rocks in the West Carson River Canyon, across Hope Valley and the Sierra Nevada summit, and on to Placerville (Hangtown then) in California. Already in 1850 some packers and walkers had started taking the Georgetown Cutoff being promoted by boosters eager for Georgetown to displace Placerville and Weberville as the California destination at the end of the trail. This route ascended the mountain from the Carson Valley in the vicinity of present Kingsbury Grade and skirted the southern end of Lake Tahoe. The grade rose too steeply for teams, and even walkers and packers found it difficult. It is "only fit for men and monkeys," observed one.[14]

Although the memory of the Donner party's ordeal and the need to cross the slippery boulders of the rushing Truckee River twenty-seven times by means of ropes diminished the desirability of Donner Pass at first, the better part of the emigrants switched to that route in mid-1849, having heard of the rigors of the Carson Canyon. The Carson route regained popularity in 1850. The easier, though lengthier, pass over the mountains was the more northerly Lassen Cutoff, by way of the glittering white playa of the Black Rock Desert. This route, however, had a bad beginning in 1848. Peter Lassen, guiding an emigrant party, became lost in the trackless, unfamiliar mountains. They wandered west, north, south, and east, until the increasingly desperate travelers threatened to hang Lassen. The party was saved only because a group of energetic and well-supplied Oregonians heading south to

Greater hardships lay ahead for the emigrants when they reached the Great Basin and the Sierra Nevada. Author's collection.

California encountered them by chance. Despite a less than promising start and much longer total mileage, an estimated eight thousand emigrants journeyed by the Lassen Cutoff in 1849, compared to slightly smaller numbers on Carson and Donner Passes.[15]

Whatever trail an emigrant chose, crossing the deserts could not be avoided. Travelers on the Carson and Truckee routes followed the Humboldt River westward across northeastern Nevada all the way to its ending at the Humboldt Sink, where they paused to prepare for the ordeal ahead. Diarist Wakeman Bryarly observed the scene:

> This marsh for three miles is certainly the liveliest place that one could witness in a lifetime. There is some two hundred and fifty wagons here all the time. Trains going out & others coming in & taking their places, is the constant order of the day. Cattle & mules by the hundreds are sur-

rounding us, in grass to their knees, all discoursing sweet music with the grinding of their jaws. Men too are seen hurrying in many different ways. . . . Some mowing, some reaping, some carrying, some packing the grass, others spreading it out to dry. . . . In fact, the joyous laugh & the familiar sound of the whetted scythe resounds from place to place & gives an air of happiness & content around that must carry the wearied travelers through to the "Promised Land."[16]

Then came the terrible—and often fatal—trials ahead for man and beast in the white sands of the waterless, grassless deserts they had feared ever since they started across the Plains. After the Humboldt Sink, the Donner and Carson trails diverged. Donner led them through areas of heavy sand and boulder-strewn hills, relieved only by a single hot springs on the way to the Truckee River; to reach Carson Pass, they had to cross the dreaded Forty Mile Desert bordering the southern edge of the Carson Sink. Underfoot, the deep, soft sand that slowed the staggering animals. All around, the omnipresent dust. And in the throat, the burning thirst. It drove the animals insane. So ravenous did the horses and mules become that after passing the desert, "they ran about wildly in the corral, picking up chips and sticks and crunching them like pipe-stems. They gnawed at the wagon boxes, tore the canvas covers, chewed ropes and driving reins, ate up a hat and some clothing of the teamsters." When they smelled a river, mules dashed through the camps of sleeping travelers all night, braying with joy. Many did not survive to dash and bray. After crossing the Forty Mile Desert, emigrant John Carr remembered: "For the last twenty miles of the desert a man could walk on dead animals all the way."[17]

Although well-managed and -supplied wagon trains came through with a minimum of hardship and relief missions from California brought fresh mounts and provisions to the starving toward the end of the season, human suffering in the deserts sometimes reached pitiful dimensions. "I never saw nor never expected to see half the suffering of man and Beast that I saw on the last part of the Road. Hundreds were begging, some killing their oxen & mules for food after they had been Rode or worked till they could go no further." Meeting wagons bearing seven men about to breathe their last, an emigrant wrote: "Men on this trip become so hardened, that they pay very little attention to anything of this kind. . . . About three men are about all you see at a burying; a man scarcely gets cold before he is in the grave."[18]

Those would be fortunate who were true *mushege*—fierce and mad enough to survive by expedients they could not have imagined in normal times. Such men clung to life by eating the rotting flesh of dead mules, which they cooked over fires fueled with lumber scavenged from abandoned wagons. At least they did not lack for wagon fuel, with five or six hundred left along the way.[19]

Travelers bound for the Carson Pass reached their first respite on the Carson River at Ragtown, which boasted a fence made from the tires of wheels from discarded wagons. Much worse lay behind the travelers, but the desert had not yet loosed its grip. Following the Carson River southwest, Bernard Reid noted: "The dust after rising a few feet high overspreads the plain like a lake of smooth muddy water. Along our line of wagons, some are completely submerged in it. Others show only their tops, which seem to go floating along like little boats in the water. Here and there the heads of men on foot stick up and glide along in rows and groups like ducks on a pond."[20]

At last they arrived in the Carson Valley, with its verdant grasses, where hundreds of animals grazed; its timbered mountain slopes, where pure, cold brooks cascaded down; and its civilized wooden buildings at Mormon Station, where a traveler could dine on grizzly steak or sage-hen soup, as well as more common fare. Virtually all emigrants perceived this valley as an Eden, though not all reached such rhapsodic heights of prose as William Kelly:

> I got into an ecstatic mood on entering it, feeling as though I stood in fairy-land; and in the blissful serenity that reigned around, feared almost to breathe, lest the mortal contamination should dissolve the deli-

Crossing of Carson River, J. J. Young, 1859. Captain J. H. Simpson's party used ropes to haul their wagon across the river on a raft, as emigrants had done in previous years. Courtesy of the Nevada State Museum, Carson City; and the National Archives, College Park, Md. (Cartographic Record, RG-77, CWMF, MISC 120–6).

cious spell by which I was entranced. It looked peacefully hallowed in its Elysian loveliness; too happy, too devine a spot for the dwelling-place of other than pure unsinful essences, where the cankers of worldly ambition could never take root or spread their baleful influences.

(Kelly, obviously, was a professional writer.) Cankers of worldly ambition had, however, emerged in the high prices charged for supplies at the trading posts strung along every mile of the valley trail. The description of Mormon Station as "a perfect skinning post" was universally echoed and widely applied to the traders in the valley by travelers.[21]

Yet the emigrants could not linger long in Eden, lest the snows fall on the final barrier before them—the towering Sierra Nevada that they called "the elephant's back." They knew the way would not be easy through the canyon cut by the West Carson River, a serpentine gap through a lofty range of mountains composed almost entirely of solid rock. There is no valley or bottoms. The walls of the mountains on each side of the creek . . . hang almost perpendicular, and probably not less than two miles high in many places. Rocks of all sizes, from the mill-stone to ten thousand tons weight have been for ages breaking loose from the heights above and tumbling down into the bottom of the cut. The waters . . . come tumbling down with a deafening roar over the piles of fallen rock & stone that have everywhere filled its channel. . . . There were so many waggons broken down and abandoned . . . that our boys gave it the name of the "Wagon Bone-yard."

Dead animals, too wasted to make the steep ascent or injured on the smooth, slippery rocks, choked the canyon. To avoid adding to the boneyard, some travelers took their wagons apart and carried them up the canyon by hand.[22]

After "this dredit place" had been conquered and a pleasant camp enjoyed in Hope Valley, the emigrants faced their final ordeal known as "the Devil's ladder"—the summit. The snow appeared "to have lain here during the lapse of ages." A traveler in early August 1850 wrote: "The road is so worn down in the snow that we cant see out the top of the bank on either hand, while setting on our mule, and at the same time with perhaps twenty feet of snow under us." By early September, more snow was falling and emigrants who had lately suffered heat and thirst in the deserts were shivering around their campfires. The Devil's ladder that loomed before them appeared almost perpendicular: "Never will I forget the profane swearing and loud whooping that was done going up this, by some teamsters. They could be heard for miles at all times on this hill and everything that could be spared was thrown away to lighten the load and even the women, I saw as we passed, had to clamber up with their children in their arms." More broken wagons and dead horses that had slipped on the ascent lay at the bottom.[23]

Besides those who swore and whooped, many surmounted the Sierra Nevada passage with considerable good humor and admired the pretty wildflowers, the huge girth of the towering pines, and the "romantic" mountain views. One party struggled through the canyon singing, "Jordan is a hard road to travel." Near the summit of Carson Pass, emigrant Lorenzo Sawyer reported "the most ludicrous combination of suffering and good humor imaginable":

> Men, ragged, dirty, and half starved, with beards long unshorn, would come hobbling along on blistered and sadly galled feet, with one boot on and the other thrown over the shoulder merrily singing "Jim crack corn, and I don't care," "O carry me back to old Virginny," "I'm going to California with my banjo on my knee" . . . as if perfectly unconscious of any uneasiness pertaining to the physical man. It was impossible to refrain from laughing at this ludicrous and incongruous exhibition of men apparently "used up" and at the same time so light and buoyant in spirits.[24]

With comparable good humor, Eliza Ann McAuley and several of her party climbed a mountain just for the fun of it while their wagons and teams toiled slowly up Donner Pass:

> [We] climbed one of the highest peaks near the road, and were well repaid for our trouble by the splendid view. . . . Turning our eyes from this, we saw the American flag floating from the summit of one of the tallest peaks. We vented our patriotism by singing "the Star Spangled Banner" and afterward enjoyed a merry game of snow ball. Turning to descend, the mountain side looked very steep and slippery, and Margaret and I were afraid to venture it. Father, who is a very active man for his age (about sixty) volunteered to show us how. . . . "Just plant your heels firmly in the snow, this way," he said, but just then, his feet flew from under him and he went sailing down the mountain side with feet and hands in the air. . . . We gave way to peals of laughter.[25]

Manifest Destiny, the westward movement of Americans from sea to shining sea, inevitable as though written in the stars. It was an old impulse that gained a new name and a great impetus in the 1840s. It meant expansion, that much was clear. But how much territory America should swallow was an issue with various answers. Perhaps only New Mexico, Oregon, and California, if such vast territories can be envisaged as the lower limit of ambition. In the minds of continental expansionists with imperial aspirations, Manifest Destiny also demanded the absorption of Canada, possibly even the entire hemisphere, including Mexico and Central America.[26]

In the minds of the gold rushers who struggled over mountains and deserts to reach the "promised land," Manifest Destiny played no discernible part. In the same way that thousands would rush to the Canadian Klondike half a century later, they came for the gold and the adventure, indifferent to what nation owned the place or what would ultimately become of it. Prentice Mulford, the San Francisco poet, later wrote: "Five years was the longest period any one expected to stay. Five years at most was to be given to rifling California of her treasures, and then that country was to be thrown aside like a used-up newspaper and the rich adventurers would spend the remainder of their days in wealth, peace, and prosperity at their Eastern homes. No one talked then of going out 'to build up the glorious State of California.' "[27]

So, too, with the seasonal traders and the plunderers. They dashed forth not to serve their nation by settling a new land but to profit from the gold rushers in their thousands, and most of them folded their makeshift tents and departed at the end of each travel season. If the gold rush abated and no more money was to be made by overcharging or robbing emigrants, they would see no reason to return.

The miners who pockmarked the sagebrush hills at Gold Canyon with their diggings saw the future in much the same way. Staying for a time to develop a fabulously rich mine was among the possibilities, of course. All the same, most hoped to get rich and get out, or, if not rich, to at least get out if the diggings failed to "prove up" and dash on to the next mining excitement, as they would do at booms across the West for the next half century.

Although a vision so vast as Manifest Destiny played no evident part in their thinking, the settlers in the valleys, by contrast, had some idea of permanence, no doubt the reason that they initially dominated the region. By any definition, they were a motley crew of renegade Mormons and old Californians who enjoyed extending the freewheeling pleasures of the great gold rush camp out on a new frontier, but they had enough expectation of remaining to make regulations governing land claims, organize a squatter government, and petition for territorial status. How their agitation would be received in Washington depended on political tides far beyond their control.[28]

The Mormon leaders in Salt Lake City most certainly foresaw a destiny for themselves, but it was a far cry from Manifest Destiny. Still scarred by the persecutions they had suffered at earlier settlements in Missouri and Illinois, they saw the safety and strength of their religious community as the immediate necessity. In 1848 the Mexican American War had closed with the cession of a vast region of the West, and in 1849 a short-lived resolution in Congress attaching the Mormon settlements to California raised the danger that they might lose control of their territory. Consequently, Brigham Young decided to organize the state of Deseret (the industrious honeybee in the *Book of Mormon*) and petition Congress for territorial status. The political machinery of the proposed state differed from the norm in other states mainly in that members of the church hierarchy would also serve as government officials—a true theocracy.[29]

Its startling feature was its enormous size, comprising not only Utah but also nearly all of Nevada and Arizona; a large portion of Colorado; parts of New Mexico, Oregon, and Idaho; and nearly the whole of southern California, including the seaport of San Diego. How Congress would receive this bid for an inland empire embracing some two hundred thousand square miles and roughly one-sixth of the present contiguous United States remained to be seen. Although Brigham Young often spoke of independence, Mormon historians have argued that the leaders of the time never contemplated secession, despite their vast territorial ambitions, only statehood. After all, when the prophet Joseph Smith had foretold that the U.S. government would be

[35]

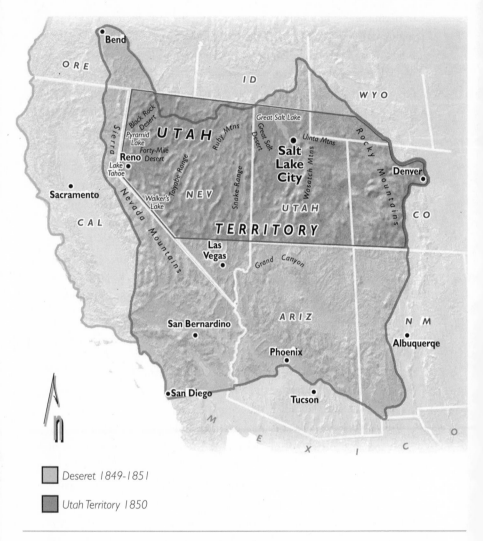

Deseret 1849-1851

Utah Territory 1850

The provisional Mormon state of Deseret (1849), Utah Territory (1850), and the present states of the region. Based on a 1940 map courtesy of the *Utah Historical Quarterly*.

"utterly overthrown and wasted" for its failure to protect the Mormons in Missouri, when Smith had revealed that the second coming would take place about 1890, when Mormons confidently expected to rule the universe in the not too distant future, territorial status would suffice for the time being.[30]

Although Manifest Destiny scarcely figured in the great folk migrations of the westward movement, it resonated loudly among eastern newspaper editors and Washington politicians, most of whom had never seen the region and displayed a "most profound" ignorance concerning it, in the words of a Mormon advocate. Ignorance posed no barrier to the grand territorial ambitions of President James Polk, however. Polk spurred the Mexican American War onward, acquired much of the West in the treaty that followed the war in 1848, and saw Texas, New Mexico, California, Oregon, and everything in between under the American flag during his single term of office, 1845–1849. In so doing, he hugely enlarged the expanse of the United States but also sharpened the rift between North and South because with so much new land to be carved up, the question of slavery in the territories became a burning issue. The South feared losing influence if the balance tipped toward the free states; the North refused to countenance the spread of slavery. Precariously, the balance teetered and held.[31]

Polk was succeeded by the hero of the Mexican American War, President Zachary Taylor, known as "Old Rough and Ready." Historians, especially the renowned Bernard DeVoto, have condemned Taylor as a crude and slovenly primitive, a general of very little brain who rode to glory on the military achievements of his subordinates, and a man of few ideas. Though his ideas may have been few, Taylor had two that he strongly maintained: California should be immediately admitted as a state, bypassing the territorial phase, and New Mexico should follow the same path when ready. Whether slave or free would be up to them. Taylor's other fixed idea was that the Mormons were outlaws and should receive neither territorial status nor statehood, despite their agitation. He even threatened a veto.[32]

Luckily for the Mormons, Old Rough and Ready overindulged on ice milk, cherries, and raw vegetables on a hot July day in 1850 and died soon after of gastroenteritis—no doubt the Mormons interpreted this as divine intervention. Brigham Young announced triumphantly, "Zachary Taylor is dead and in hell, and I am glad of it." Taylor's successor, Millard Fillmore, one of the most invisible of presidents, was far more sympathetic to the Mormons. Under the Compromise of 1850, California became an instant state, bypassing the territorial phase as Taylor had wished, New Mexico became a territory, and the Mormons also gained territorial status on September 9, 1850, under the name of Utah preferred by Congress. They did not, however, gain the vast domain they had claimed for Deseret. They would be forced to content themselves with Utah and most of Nevada plus scraps of Colorado and Wyoming.[33]

The settlers on the eastern slope figured not at all in the mighty decisions rumbling through Washington that affected their fate. Indeed, that profound ignorance of the West that prevailed in the East probably plumbed the greatest depths where their corner of the world was concerned. In maps the landmass from Salt Lake to the Sierra Nevada often appeared as an empty space, perhaps labeled the "Great Interior Basin of California" or "terra incognita," perhaps as the "immenses plaines sablonneuses" (the great sandy plains). Some maps depicted features that never were, the fanciful Santa Buenaventura River rushing across the desert on its way to the Pacific Ocean, or a mighty east-west mountain chain in a land where the ranges run north-south. One map showed the eastern slope as part of the new state of California, as the settlers heartily would have wished it to be. Cartography aside, the great basin was admittedly an empty space with a population in the hundreds in 1854, compared to 92,600 in California in 1850 and perhaps 40,000 in Utah ten years later. Although the old standard of a population of 60,000 for territorial status had long since lapsed into desuetude, the idea that a few hundred would suffice must have sounded to many like the ravings of madmen.[34]

The drive on the eastern slope for freedom from Mormon rule by annexation to California had failed, partly through concerns that if California were too large and unwieldy it might be subdivided to create a southern California slave state. Yet despite a ridiculously small population, several elements favored the drive on the eastern slope for territorial status. The slope had an aggressive group of settlers, and in many states local agitation played a large part in winning territorial status. Initially, at least, opposition to Mormon control served as the great unifier that kept factionalism to a minimum. Moreover, the settlers' dislike of Mormon rule would find a good deal of sympathy in Congress, where anti-Mormon prejudice could easily be stirred. Another element in their favor was congressional reluctance to create excessively large states. Though this had helped wither their hopes of annexation to California, it could now work in their behalf because a bloated Utah that encompassed Nevada could certainly be seen as excessively large.[35]

Finally, Congress had shown sympathy for the communication problems of isolated communities, and the eastern slope unquestionably met that standard. The transportation and communication revolution in rail, steam, macadamized roads, and telegraphs made the incorporation of the West into the union a theoretical possibility by 1850, but the days when Cincinnati to New York meant a three-week journey had not been forgotten, and the new improvements as yet had no relevance in the Great Basin. When winter snows closed the Sierra Nevada, communication with California ended until spring. Salt Lake City lay five hundred miles eastward, and despite some improvements the journey remained slow and difficult in summer and rare in winter. Just how difficult was illustrated by George Chorpenning's heroic struggle to fulfill his government mail contract in 1851–1852. Chorpenning lost his partner, Absalom Woodward, and two mail carriers to Indian attacks in the Great Basin; other carriers barely escaped with their lives but not the mail. On a two-month winter journey in which their mules froze to death in blizzards, another mail party divided the frozen mule meat among themselves and continued on foot. Discouraged, Chorpenning switched to a southern route through San Bernardino in 1853–1854.[36]

This change left the eastern slope in undisturbed winter solitude until 1856, when the hardy Norwegian John A. "Snowshoe" Thompson began making ninety-mile mail runs in two or three days across the snowbound Sierra Nevada between the Carson Valley and Placerville on skis. His mailbags weighed as much as sixty to eighty pounds; he wore no overcoat, carried no blankets, and if he rested at all he built a fire in a tree stump to warm his feet while he lay on a bed of pine boughs. He never lost his way. In the words of an early historian, "He courted, rather than feared, the perils of the mountains when visited by their fiercest storms; and the wild rage of a midnight tempest could not disconcert or drive him from his path." Still, communication with the outside world depended almost entirely on one lone skier.[37]

If isolation, anti-Mormon prejudice, and agitation could be turned to good account, territorial status may have seemed not so wild a dream as 1854 drew to a close on the western periphery of the Mormon empire.

3

The Cursed Black Stuff

GOLD CANYON miners remembered a Mexican in 1853 who had pointed excitedly upward toward Sun Peak and exclaimed, "Mucho plata." Even if they had understood the stream of Spanish that poured from his lips, they would have been supremely uninterested. It was gold they wanted, just like the gold of California, only gold. Thus they continued placering with their rockers for gold specks worth two or five dollars a day in the narrow declivity between the sagebrush hills, while higher, on the slope below Sun Peak, the silver treasure of the great Comstock Lode worth nearly $350 million remained undisturbed. These miners had undoubtedly prospected higher up the canyon looking for the source of the placer gold, but they had not looked very hard. William Dolman, walking over the future Comstock in 1858, saw no signs of serious mineral exploration, nor did he pause to dig.[1]

Hispanics were more astute. As early as 1850 an emigrant noted several Mexican pack companies driving donkeys en route from California to Gold Canyon, where they twirled the placer sands in wooden bowls, scraping out the golden flecks with horn spoons. However, expensive supplies and lack of transportation compelled them to leave after a few weeks. They reportedly saw traces of silver but ignored them because they knew the necessary capital to develop a silver mine would be out of reach.[2]

The first of record to recognize the real value of Comstock silver was "Old Frank" Antonio. Early historians have described him as Mexican, but this may indicate nothing more than the Anglo practice of labeling everyone from south of the border a Mexican. A relevant letter relates that Antonio went to Gold Canyon "in company with" Mexican miners, which may imply that he himself was not Mexican. Henry Comstock, one of the early prospectors in the region, and author Charles Shinn call him Brazilian, which seems plausible. Old Frank came in 1852–1853 with a small group of just five Mexican companions traveling eastward from El Dorado County, California. In a long-lost manuscript, forty-niner Francis J. Hoover related that while pursuing his stolen horse Old Frank took a specimen from a "table-land running north and south and broadside to the sunrise." Unlike so many others, Old Frank saw something more than immediate returns from gold dust. He knew precious silver when he saw it.[3]

Another to recognize and value the silver in the region was a member of an old and aristocratic Italian family, Count Leonetto Cipriani. The count had led a virtually operatic life. As a teenage aide to an officer in the French army in Algeria, he fell in love with a beautiful captive Italian girl in the dey's harem and brought her home, where he secreted her in a small hotel. Learning of the affair, his family ended it, and the heartbroken girl drowned herself. Cipriani went on to fight for Italian independence and undertake various political activities in which his intimacy with the Bonapartes served him well. The gold rush focused his attention on the United States. He first traveled to California by sea. Then, in 1853, at age forty, he decided to drive a large herd of five hundred cattle and six hundred oxen, as well as horses, mules, and cargo, overland for sale in California as a business venture. He organized his party on the basis of "strict discipline and absolute obedience" and read the men their orders, which included the proviso that deserters fortunate enough to be spared execution would be chained.[4]

Count Leonetto Cipriani, the prospector as aristocrat.
Courtesy of the President and Fellows of Harvard College,
from HOLLIS, no. 004530162, Cambridge, Mass.

The count proceeded ahead of the herd by covered wagon with a few companions. While resting his mules by the Carson River, he decided to take a ride north and "perceived a vein or metallic stratum which had all the appearances of being silver." He took a few samples to be assayed in San Francisco. "It was found that the mineral contained 20,000 dollars worth of silver per ton," Cipriani wrote in his diary. "But at that time in the gold country, silver was too poor a metal to deserve attention. Everyone refused to give it any importance."[5]

Count Cipriani accepted this verdict, to his subsequent regret. Reflecting on the past from his castle in Corsica, he wrote: "When a man is not destined by Providence to make a fortune, there is no use finding gold or silver mines; he might just as well be finding mud. All I would have had to do was return to Carson right away, where I would have wintered with my trustworthy companions, to gather within a few months enough silver to make at least 100,000 dollars." The count believed he had taken his sample from the site of the fabulous Comstock Lode.[6]

Meanwhile, Old Frank encountered the same indifference to his silver samples. The only exceptions were the Grosh brothers, Ethan Allen (the elder, who signed himself as Allen or E. A. in the invaluable letters to their father that record their experiences) and Hosea Ballou. These two were different from most of the prospectors dotting the hills of Gold Canyon, indeed, very different from the founding father James Finney, pickled in his burrow. Sons of a New England teacher and Universalist minister, they were sober, industrious, and too single-minded to fraternize much; the others were more convivial, devotees of the excitement and brotherhood of the prospecting way of life, celebrants on every occasion and no occasion with a round of drinks, and often no more industrious than they had to be. The Grosh brothers had actually studied metallurgy, at least in books; the rest usually picked up what they knew from comrades, rumor, superstition, hard experience, anything but science. It would seem that the Groshes possessed every ingredient for success in mining except the most important one—luck.[7]

When Allen set his heart upon joining the California gold rush, his parents insisted that he take his younger brother, Hosea, because they regarded their oldest son as something of a wild card. They hoped that Hosea's "strong caution, prudence, and patient, cheerful, steady philosophy" would temper Allen's "impulsiveness." The two brothers embarked with a company of forty-niners from Reading, Pennsylvania, two specks among more than eighty thousand Americans to make the journey by land and sea in that year, many with only the dimmest idea of what lay ahead. Crossing Mexico by way of Tampico and Mazatlán, Hosea became seriously ill with dysentery, and their company soon quarreled and broke up. The brothers lingered long in San Francisco, frequently bedridden with various illnesses and sometimes beachcombing for their dinners. Not until June 1850 did they finally arrive in the gold country. "Health, youth, strong arms, & stout hearts, and two years experience. What more could we ask? We are in California!" wrote Allen at the beginning of 1851. During their remaining years, as their letters to their father attest, poverty, hardship, and failure would darken their exuberant hopes to the depths of despair.[8]

But until that time arrived, they clung to the dream of a "princely fortune." Because normal employment lacked the promise of a grand bonanza, they turned down well-paying jobs as clerks and the like, in which they would have made more in a couple of months than they ever made in mining. Aside from the invention of miraculous machines, the other path to riches that they attempted was a farm, which, instead of expanding to a large-scale operation with plenty of stock, predictably failed because they were inexperienced at farming and did not persist in the enterprise. Had they gained the great fortune of their imaginations, their dreams for spending it were unselfish and fairly modest—a piano for their musically talented sister and a halcyon colony in California where all the Groshes of their extended family, from grandfather to little ones, would live in prosperity and happiness: "The plan is to get our own family [and Uncle] Pinckney's together with some of the rest out here & and settle down in one year we can raise every thing we need in the gardening & farming keep a little stock & have it increase. In this way we will have every thing necessary & keep growing from competence to wealth here in the mines. We will have market in our neighborhood for all we have to spare for many years." After discussing their future orchards, Allen added: "If we became wealthy we would buy other ranches below & raise everything the country can produce. All this will follow easily if once our family settle in this country even if our mines fail of which there is no probability."[9]

Unfortunately, the probability could not be so lightly dismissed. When they at last reached the gold country in the early summer of

1850, the brothers placered a little gold, and their hope to discover a rich vein of gold flared again and again, only to be dashed. Some of the time they lived off the land like mountain men by hunting. At the same time, they toiled away at inventing a machine that would bring the "princely fortune" of their dreams. Their grandfather had been "mechanically inclined," and they hailed from a section of the country that abounded in hopeful inventors. In San Francisco, before they had ever placered in the Sierra Nevada, they were hard at work upon a gold-washing machine: "The model is just completed and will be tried tomorrow or next day I am more sanguine than ever—I do not see how it can fail—and if it succeeds it will be a fortune to us sure." Fail it did, but the brothers were not discouraged. Soon they waxed enthusiastic about other impractical mechanical improvements. After these also failed, they would begin building their last and most harebrained scheme of all—their perpetual-motion machine.[10]

When Old Frank told the Groshes about his silver discovery sometime in the winter of 1852–1853, they were ready for a change. They had failed at California gold mining, they had failed at ranching, and they had failed at the invention of miraculous machines: "We are kept so busy climbing the hills of adversity that we are conyinually out of breath." Now, on the basis of "good and reliable information," they planned to pull up stakes and head for the east side of the Sierra Nevada as soon as the mountains became "passable for animals." Nonetheless, it was mid-July before they finally wrote their father, "Ho! For the Mountains!" and set off.[11]

They did not head immediately for Gold Canyon but spent almost three months prospecting around the eastern Sierra Nevada, sometimes in the vicinity of Lake Tahoe (then Lake Bigler), which suggests other informants besides Old Frank. All the same, they ultimately named their California silver mining company after him and later called him "the one who sent us over the mountains in 1853," which indicates the primacy of his guidance. Probably, they arrived in Gold Canyon no sooner than mid-October, when the creek that dried to a

The ill-fated Grosh brothers, Hosea Ballou *(left)* and Ethan Allen.
Courtesy Nevada Historical Society, Reno.

trickle during the summer months began to flow down the canyon again and washing placer gold with rockers and Long Toms became feasible once more. Placer miners needed water pouring into their rockers to wash gold dust and nuggets through the box to be trapped in the riffles below while the screen on top caught pebbles and rocks; the Long Tom (an inclined trough up to twelve feet long) operated on similar principles, often with several men occupied in shoveling in gravel, breaking the clods, stirring the mixture, and keeping the water flowing. The estimated number of miners earning about five dollars a day from placering in 1853 shifted according to the season, from ninety in the fall and winter to twenty during the summer. When the crop season ended, ranchers from the Carson Valley would arrive in Gold Canyon to mine.[12]

In Gold Canyon the Groshes found a way of life so primitive, with miners "about two or three years behind the age," that the California diggings seemed civilized by contrast. And this assessment applied to more than mining technology. The scattered prospectors in the sagebrush hills lining the canyon lived in brush shelters like the Indians or in tents in summer and moved into stone huts in winter. Their only amusements were gambling and drinking at the station house at the foot of the canyon or at the combination store, saloon, and bowling alley at Maiden Bar a mile and a quarter farther up. The brothers busied themselves "getting up a house, (which is considerable of a job where there is no timber) & getting fixed &c trying to make expenses." They had nonetheless recovered their optimism. Hosea wrote: "There is certainly the best chance to [do] well here of any where I have been."[13]

A big gap in the Grosh letters ensues, due to either difficulties in communication from the eastern slope or the destruction of some letters. In November 1854 Allen reported that they were "once more in California, after passing through trials and hardships which five years ago would have sent us to our graves." They believed that they had discovered a silver mine in Gold Canyon: "The one we found was the black silver ore, if silver it was, in masses large as your fist. We were so hard pressed by poverty while on the other side that we never tested it."[14]

Yet they had not persisted. They would pass almost two years in the California gold diggings, scraping a bare living and too poor to afford a horse or a mineralogy book, before they finally returned to their silver mine.[15] Along the eastern side of the high, barren mountains, concealed by wash, the Comstock Lode that one day would be the making of Nevada still slept.

The Mormons Take Charge, 1855

O LONGER did the wagons roll west in a continuous stream of dust; no longer did the myriad scythes of hay-makers flash in the Humboldt Sink; no longer did the mountains ring with the curses and songs of men struggling up the Carson Canyon. By 1854 the human avalanche of 1849 on the California trails had fallen by more than half to an estimated twelve thousand, but the practice of driving large herds of stock, as Count Cipriani had done, increased. One party lost five hundred cattle in an early snowstorm on Carson Pass. Trail accounts largely echo those of earlier years—the same delight in the lushness of the Carson Valley after the deserts, the same difficulties along the way: "There was no such thing as roads. Just the wheel tracks of wagons of former years." In 1855, following conflict with the Sioux near Fort Laramie, fear diminished the numbers of earlier years to a trickle of only a few hundred.[1]

Although the opportunities to trade with the emigrants (or rob them, as did the Reddens) had shriveled, a few nascent communities still clung to the bosom of the Sierra Nevada. At the end of the Forty Mile Desert, Ragtown retained its old appearance, a few pieces of canvas stretched over poles. At the mouth of Gold Canyon, a one-family log house, station, and smithy formed the nucleus of future Dayton, but the site had largely been left behind for Johntown, a store owned by the Cossers around which a few shacks gathered, as the miners in their nomadic fashion followed the placer gold farther up Gold Canyon. In 1855 their numbers peaked at about two hundred and their estimated returns at $118,000; both would drop sharply during the following years. In 1856 Chinese laborers would be brought to the initial settlement to dig a ditch, which failed to function as planned because water stubbornly refused to run uphill. The Chinese decided to remain to wash the last traces of placer gold, and for a time future Dayton became known as Chinatown. It was officially renamed Dayton in 1861 to compensate surveyor John Dayton for his labors. The Carson Valley, a vista of green meadows and handsome ranches, kept its place as the center of population and influence, with perhaps two hundred residents and a squatter government given to occasional agitation. An 1854 Carson Valley directory listed eighteen trading posts between Mormon Station and Hope Valley, several offering stock to exchange and, at the hot springs, the luxury of a bathhouse, as well as grass and liquors. Although the valley now boasted two sawmills, the early settlers put the materials at hand to good use, as in the ranch house constructed from the beds of wrecked wagons.[2]

Some of the Carson Valley's memorable cast of characters from the early days remained, among them Lucky Bill Thorington, gambling, succoring destitute emigrants with acts of kindness, and rapidly evolving into a successful businessman, with the acquisition of Reese's ranch, stock, and inn at Mormon Station as well as his claim to the Eagle Valley ranch and a half interest in a bridge and the "Old Emigrant Road" to satisfy a $23,000 loan. He had brought his son and his wife, the beautiful dark-eyed Maria, probably already slipping into insanity. Although it is not clear just when his scandalous affair with another woman began, Lucky Bill was a family man after his own fashion. He had not institutionalized his mad wife, divorced her, or left her behind in what would later become known as a "Washoe divorce." For better or worse, he kept her with him. Lucky Bill's close friend Uncle Billy Rogers also remained for the time being and started a pack train service between Mormon Station and Placerville, but he was not immune to the restlessness endemic among the old frontiersmen. A popular bon vivant like Lucky Bill had few enemies in the Carson Valley until his growing prominence made him a target. Three of the few who would one day become bitter enemies had just moved into the Clear Creek Ranch, Richard Sides, L. B. Abernathy, and John M. Baldwin.[3]

In 1851 several placer miners from California, Joseph Barnard, Frank Barnard, Frank Hall, W. L. Hall, A. J. Rollins, and George Follensbye had killed an eagle north of the Carson Valley, over the low sagebrush hills and beyond the shallow cup of Jacks Valley where the Washo used to camp and the Reddens had made their base. They named the place Eagle Valley and erected a station there. Nonetheless, the future capital of Nevada lacked the meadows and prosperous ranches that delighted emigrants in the Carson Valley and played a lesser role until it attracted the attention of ambitious men.[4]

In the spring of 1854, the flamboyant figure who was to be the most notorious desperado in the region made his debut with a jingling of Mexican spurs. Sam Brown, then about twenty-three, was a happy-go-lucky pleasant fellow when sober and a demon when drunk, which was often. With his long, curling sandy-red hair, hazel-gray eyes, ruddy complexion, goatee, and ability to move quick as a cat despite his heft and breadth, he made a strong impression—and probably intended to. At a vaguely described location, no doubt Mormon Station or Eagle Station, "Long-Haired" Brown and another gambler known as "One-Eyed" Gray argued over their cards. Brown struck the one-eyed man with his revolver, then shot him in the head. Gray died about two weeks later, and Brown vamoosed to California, though he had little to fear in the absence of law on the eastern slope.[5]

It was not the region's first homicide. Aside from the Donner party stabbing in 1846 and violent incidents between Indians and whites, an early historian records a homicide in 1851 and another in 1853. Nor was it Brown's first homicide. That may have occurred in Texas before he joined the California gold rush to become a professional gambler and an even more professional desperado, with two California homicides to his discredit. He would be unavoidably detained in Califor-

nia—in San Quentin, to be exact—after stabbing two "Chilenos" in another gambling dispute in 1855. But he would be back after his release
to cut a wide swath.[6]

Northward, across another set of sagebrush hills, lay Washoe Valley,
the next in the chain. Although the mighty forested mountains cul-
minating in the Sierra Nevada also thrust from the valley floor to the
west and grayer desert hills bounded the valley to the east, Washoe
Valley differed from the others in some respects. Its climate was
colder, making it a true alpine valley, it contained a large shallow lake
abounding in trout, and no branches of the California trails passed
through it, resulting in no emigrant traffic and no traders. Washoe did,
however, contain a few ranches, the first belonging to a settler named
Clark so charmed by the beauty of this valley where the white clover
grew amazingly tall that he named his place "the Garden of Eden." His
paradise lasted only briefly. A year later conflict with the Washo compelled him to abandon his ranch.[7]

Across another boundary of low hills cupping pocket-size Pleasant
Valley came the Truckee Meadows (present Reno). Many emigrants
passed through on the Donner Trail or cut north on the loop of the
Beckwourth route, but the influx of traders and ranchers lagged behind the Carson Valley. H. H. Jameson, a former Carson Valley agent
for the Chorpenning mail enterprise and possibly an early arrival with
the Reese party, may have come from the Carson Valley as early as
1852, though emigrant diaries fail to confirm his presence. Two other
traders opened up shop in the Meadows in 1854, whether as competi-
tors of Jameson or purchasers of his setup is not clear. Flooding and
Indian stock thefts had retarded settlement.[8]

Honey Lake Valley, the last cluster of settlement on the eastern
slope, was separated from the others by more than sixty miles of
deserts and mountains of the Indian country west of Pyramid Lake.
Although no one realized it yet, this valley lay over the California state
line. In the summer of 1853, a heavyhearted thirty-one-year old widower named Isaac Roop saddled his horse and headed east on Nobles

Road through the Sierra Nevada to Honey Lake Valley. Born in Maryland, he had moved west to Ohio with his family and operated a saw- and gristmill. A neighboring girl, Nancy Gardner, married him when both were eighteen, taught him to read and write for he had little education, bore him three children, and died suddenly of typhoid fever after ten years of marriage. The life Isaac Roop had known ended with her death. Leaving his children with their grandparents, he followed an older brother to California, but he did not emerge from the experience a tough frontiersman. The influence of his father, a devout Dunker, showed in his idealism and his simple goodness.[9]

In Honey Lake Valley, Roop took out the first land claim and built a log house. Though he may have wintered on the west side of the Sierra Nevada during that first year, he opened a trading station in 1854 and kept a book in which the passing emigrants registered. More than five hundred came through by mid-August, and the Paiutes visited amicably, led by Chief Winnemucca, with whom Roop formed a cordial relationship. A handful of other settlers joined Roop, but to their regret, white women were few and far between. No more than fifteen could be counted in the entire region from the Carson Valley to Honey Lake. One resident wrote: "Girls are very scarce non coming of any amount. . . . It is no good for a man to be a lone Verely." Any emigrant party that included these scarce and fondly remembered rarities was eagerly pressed to join a dance.[10]

In the spring of 1852, two years after Congress granted Utah territorial status, Utah officials drew a series of straight lines across the map. Straight as the streets of Mormon towns, straight as the lines of poplars along their lanes, straight as the iron bars of a cage, these seven extensions of Utah counties marched across the lands to the west, bending neither for settlements nor for topography. Had these counties been anything more than abstractions on the map, they would have caused major inconvenience to the settlers on the eastern slope because anyone needing to undertake one of the myriad transactions of official business would have been obliged to make a lengthy

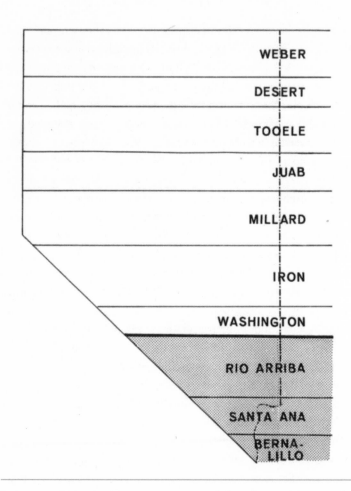

WEBER

DESERT

TOOELE

JUAB

MILLARD

IRON

WASHINGTON

RIO ARRIBA

SANTA ANA

BERNA-
LILLO

In 1852 Utah's territorial government extended Utah counties across future
Nevada. From John Koontz, *Political History of Nevada*, 1965, p. 37.

and tedious journey of more than five hundred miles. All the same, the straight lines on the map accomplished their intended purpose. They demonstrated that Utah was organizing the western portion of its vast realm, a move no doubt intended to countermand the agitation in 1851 by the squatter government in the Carson Valley for separate territorial status.[11]

The agitation had only increased with an 1853 petition from forty-three Carson Valley residents appealing to the California legislature to annex the eastern slope. Clearly, more forceful action was needed to suppress these rebellious subjects. In January 1854, the Utah legislature created Carson County, a twenty thousand–square-mile monster covering the western portion of their territory, with Mormon Station as its county seat. Carson County would have a U.S. judge, probate judge, marshal, and representative in the Utah legislature. In 1856 Utah would again redraw the county map, extending Carson County to the Oregon border and creating two northern counties on paper, although both remained attached to a county within the borders of present-day Utah for all practical purposes and contained hardly any settlers.[12]

More agitation. Instead of bringing their problems to the nominal government in Utah, the squatter government drafted their own constitution and held another meeting in May 1854 to set rules on water rights. If the eastern slope was to remain firmly within Utah's grip and the California annexation movement was to be quashed, the obvious answer would be to transform the region into a Mormon colony. The lessons of history were not entirely encouraging. Where the Mormons had lived among "Gentiles" in Missouri and Illinois, the result had been persecution and enforced flight. One of the great attractions of the Salt Lake Valley to their leaders had been the absence of other people. Yet the sparse settlers on the eastern slope could easily be swamped by an influx of Mormon newcomers, and the widespread Mormon colonization effort of which this would be a part had enjoyed stunning success. During the decade following their own arrival in the Salt Lake Valley in 1847, the Mormons started ninety-six colonies, beginning with the inner circle of valleys near Salt Lake, extending steadily outward, and establishing a string of settlements along the "Mormon Corridor" to connect with their California colony at San Bernardino. In May 1855 Brigham Young dispatched a twenty-eight-man mission to establish a vital link along the corridor at Las Vegas that would serve as a gathering place for California Mormons, for missionaries going forth, and for converts arriving from the Pacific missions. Though the men erected mesquite fences, planted crops, built a fort of adobe bricks, mined lead at nearby Potosi, and endeavored to convert the Southern Paiutes, they were discontented in the heat and desolation of the desert. Their leader, William Bringhurst, found it necessary to reprove them for "grumbling, fault finding, laziness, and cussing around." From the outset, until Young terminated it in February 1857, the Las Vegas mission remained entirely separate and disconnected from the Mormons on the eastern slope.[13]

Young also envisaged the Carson Valley as "mainly a funnel" for arriving converts from California and Oregon on their way to Utah, in the phrase of historian Leonard Arrington. Young declared he was not "desirous that any should remain at Carson Valley who wish to come here. These places are only fixed that those who are disposed may be gathered and not left to wander like sheep without a shepherd." To accomplish this difficult and dangerous mission, Young appointed one of the twelve apostles of the church, Orson Hyde.[14]

Despite his conversion to the church when he and it were young, his high rank in the church hierarchy, and his outstanding record as a missionary in Europe and a colonizer, a taint of unorthodoxy clung to Orson Hyde, as was also true of other Mormons prominent in the history of a region notorious as a hotbed of apostates. Abner Blackburn had been an admitted skeptic; John Reese, as a settler delicately put it, was only "partially connected with the church"; and Orson Hyde had apostatized in 1838. He soon returned to the fold and was restored to his position as one of the twelve, though stripped of his seniority. All was not quite forgiven, however. Young publicly ridiculed and chas-

Orson Hyde organized a Mormon settlement on the
eastern slope. Courtesy Nevada Historical Society, Reno.

tised him on occasion as "a stink in [my] nostrils." If an anti-Mormon
polemic can be believed, "Orson Hyde's cupidity is too well known; his
apostasy in 1838 too well remembered, and his impetuosity too much
dreaded."[15]

Hyde set off for the Carson Valley in June 1855 at age fifty, an old
man by the standards of the young gold rushers. Young had appointed
him probate judge, as well as spiritual head and organizer of the
colony to be. His mission had nothing to do with the Mormon colony
of 1855–1857 in the Las Vegas Valley, a separate and distinct undertaking. In keeping with the usual Mormon practice, Hyde traveled in advance of the colonists to scope out the eastern slope in company with
other newly selected officials for Carson County—U.S. judge George
Stiles and U.S. marshal J. L. Haywood—and thirty-six guards and mis-

sionaries, all men. Fearful of Indians, notwithstanding his guards, Hyde related that "we have to sleep with one eye open, one foot out of bed, a rifle in one hand and a revolver in the other." Reaching the Carson Valley, the apostle would have his work cut out for him. Already in 1853 Mormon bishop Edwin Wooley had reported: "As to Mormonism, I can't find it here. If the name remains, the Spirit has fled. I have my doubts whether Mormonism can exist in the country."[16]

Nor had the Spirit returned since 1853. In one of his many letters to Brigham Young, Hyde reported, "There are many mormons here, but I fear not Saints." Nonetheless, he liked the land before him: "This [the Carson Valley] is a beautiful valley; and if I say anything about it, I must speak in its praise. There are also many valleys in this vicinity rich and fertile sufficient to make a state or an empire." Apart from participating in an October 27 meeting of several Mormons to allocate water rights in Gold Canyon, mainly for mining purposes, he had nothing to do with the Gold Canyon miners, at one point remarking that he "didn't propose to mix himself up with any Gentile messes." But he rapidly exceeded his instructions for the eastern slope, in his eyes more than a gathering place for the wandering sheep but, rather, a potential agricultural empire.[17]

Dissatisfied with the 1852 survey establishing that the eastern slope lay outside the California boundary line, Hyde insisted upon a new survey, which he presently undertook in conjunction with the California officials he prodded into action. It reaffirmed the earlier survey, to the settlers' disappointment and Hyde's gratification. When it became evident that his mission would last longer than originally planned, Hyde decided that he wanted a wife with him, and unlike the wistful yearners in the Honey Lake Valley, he could send for one by mail order. He asked Young to send him a wife, hinting that a new one would not be unwelcome: "The chances to get a wife here are not very many even if a man wanted to get one in this country. *Women* are scarce here, and good ones are scarcer still." Instead of recruiting a new one, Young packed up one of Hyde's old wives, Mary Ann. Fortunately, she was there to nurse him after a near fatal attempt to cross the Sierra Nevada in December left him with severely frostbitten feet.[18]

As soon as the weather allowed, Hyde continued his preparations. Stumping about on his damaged feet in moccasins and "not idle a bit," he quickly began surveying the valleys and making land claims for the colonists to come, mainly in Washoe Valley and the Truckee Meadows, since settlers had already filled most of the Carson Valley. He prided himself on deceiving the settlers into believing that his interest centered on the Honey Lake Valley in order to forestall a rush of speculative claims and a rise in land prices (Mormon practice approved "lying for the Lord" to protect the interests of the church). Reaching an accommodation with the Washo, whose hostility had retarded settlement in Washoe Valley, Hyde made this spot the center of the new colony and later established his own ranch and sawmill there. He also laid out a town plan for Mormon Station, which he renamed Genoa in honor of Columbus.[19]

In the spring of 1856, the assigned colonists, estimated at 200–250, arrived. In keeping with the pattern of Mormon colonization, many had been selected because they had useful skills as butchers, tanners, weavers, brick makers, and so forth to contribute to the new colony, but there may have been an element of punishment in the assignment as well (as perhaps also for Hyde). A virulently anti-Mormon author of the time recounts an anecdote in which a Salt Lake City storekeeper who unwisely tried to bargain over the price of a stove with a Mormon elder found himself forced to sell his stock and assigned to the Carson Valley colony.[20]

Even if they had not run afoul of influential elders, some colonists saw their mission as a great trial. Hating the towering mountains that rose sheer from the valley floor, the tall trees, and the small primitive settlements, Mary Jane Phippen urged her family not to follow: "Father talk no more of coming to this place I would rather have one acher of land in Salt Lake City than the hole of Carson Valey. [Y]ou have a good home and I beg of you to stay there. . . . There is plenty of

Jentiles here cursing and severing gambling and horse racing is the principal business of the day." More than a month later her opinion had not improved: "This is surely the most God forsaken place that I ever was in in all my life." Dissatisfaction among the settlers became a major problem for Hyde: "Many of the brethren are dissatisfied and act childish. . . . They want their bread and butter all spread for them." He ascribed their grumbling to the lack of "comforts and conveniency" in a new country.[21]

Nonetheless, the problem for Hyde that loomed far larger than the complaints of the colonists was the opposition of many Gentile settlers to Mormon rule. This had been apparent from the beginning. In 1852 a traveler had reported to Brigham Young: "The citizens of this valley declare in language too strong to utter that they will no longer be governed or tried by Mormon law . . . and declare they will pay no taxes that are levied on them from that source." Upon his arrival, Hyde found the settlers "much divided," some favoring government by Utah, most preferring California, and others pinning their hopes on a separate territory. Hyde himself would not have minded two territories— provided that the Mormons controlled both—and Young concurred with this view.[22]

No doubt, Hyde's manifestly political activities exacerbated the antagonism toward Mormons. He wrote to Young: "I would say secure, secure for growing and increasing Utah. . . . As an agent for a great people I say that I want it secured. The timber, the water, the grass, the fish, the remarkably healthful climate and rich soil are elements of vital importance to the increasing strength and glory of Zion." And secure he did. His involvement in the survey that placed the eastern slope outside California and his numerous land claims for the incoming colonists were well known among the settlers. Suspecting California of an underhanded effort to annex the eastern slope, Hyde may not have been entirely wrong. Why would California, despite a definitive survey, send a tax collector to the eastern slope to gather payments that residents denied to Utah? Hyde's suggestion that governance be conducted with a light hand showed that he himself was not above guile. He also postponed organizing a militia as Young had directed, well aware of the likely reaction among the settlers. At the same time, he strongly urged Brigham Young to send more colonists, especially *voters*, to overwhelm the Gentiles in elections and occupy the empty spaces that might otherwise be filled by Gentiles from California. He proposed one hundred men traveling west in early spring with sealed instructions: "It is necessary for a strong force to be here. The country is worthy, but Devils will reign unless we get in so thick that there is no chance for them."[23]

The creation of Carson County and the arrival of Utah officials to administer it hardly mollified the settlers opposed to Mormon rule. Judge Stiles, an apostate detested by many Mormons, convened the first district court in early September. Shortly afterward he ended the session and departed for Utah with the marshal because the court had little business other than the naturalization of new citizens. Hyde's influence already figured in the election he called in the autumn of 1855. All the Mormon candidates he chose won, confirming the settlers' fears of Mormon domination, but several old settlers gained office. That any candidate stood for the office of sheriff is surprising because the eastern slope's first two lawmen had been shot. In 1852 N. R. Haskill invited Sheriff William Byrnes to join him in an exhibition of target shooting at a tent trading station at the mouth of Gold Canyon. Byrnes, a former Texas Ranger renowned for his prowess with guns, emptied his revolver at the target. Haskill, for reasons unknown, emptied *his* revolver at Byrnes. Amazingly, the hardy young sheriff recovered, and Haskill fled to California. Byrnes later dropped a hint that on his numerous trips to California he had finally caught up with Haskill. The eastern slope's next lawman, Constable Joseph P. Barnard, was shot and killed in 1853 by a trader near Clear Creek when he attempted to ride his horse into the trading post.[24]

In addition to these memorable episodes in which devils reigned, the fundamental conflict between settlers and Mormons continued.

The settlers sent a petition to the California legislature in 1855 asking to be annexed to California, which the legislature approved, but Congress failed to act. Not one to be outdone, Hyde worked up a counterpetition. This, in turn, provoked a counterpetition from the ladies of the valleys (all fifteen of them, presumably) protesting a government that forced polygamy upon women and compelled them to associate with a "Scarlet Lady" (Mary Ann). Indeed, spiritual leader Orson Hyde's marital history, past and future, confirmed their darkest imaginings. Although they evidently knew that Mary Ann was not his only wife, they could not yet know that upon his return to Utah at age fifty-two he would marry a sixteen year old and would continue to accumulate young wives as he grew older. He may have considered a plenitude of wives to be a status symbol validating his high position as a Mormon leader.[25]

In the summer of 1856, the Mormon-Gentile balance had shifted slightly when U.S. Judge William Drummond arrived and convened court in a barn with the prostitute who accompanied him seated at his side. In a closely watched case concerning payment owed Thomas Knott for construction of a sawmill and a gristmill for John Reese, Judge Drummond ruled in favor of Knott (a non-Mormon) over Reese (a semi-, demi-, quasi Mormon), reversing a previous decision by Hyde in his capacity as probate judge. Hyde thought Drummond prejudiced against Mormons and believed the judge had been bribed with the gift of a horse. Indeed, Drummond's declaration that "money is my god" may have been interpreted as a hint. After much litigation, Knott would be denied payment for the mill and turn in impotent fury against the Mormons, whom he would blame three years later for the most grievous tragedy of his life.[26]

The tension tightened. As the August election approached, the settlers termed their office seekers the "human ticket," as opposed to the "Mormon ticket." Backed by the votes of the new colonists, the Mormon ticket swept the election, and the settlers began to hold anti-Mormon meetings and to resist by extralegal methods. Mormon co-

[62]

lonist Sylvester Phippen wrote a colorful description of an attempted sheriff's sale of the Richard Sides ranch in Eagle Valley to satisfy a debt owed to Reese: "By and by the Sheriff expected a row and took down a pretty larg Possy But on ariving at the Ranch thay found the Rowdes well armed with guns and Pistols and equal if not Superior to the Sheriff's Possy in numbers They swore they would shout the Sheriff the minute he offered the property for sail there was a few Knockdowns a good deal of swairing don and whiskey drank and finely ended in the Sheriff postponing the Sail." The next effort to sell the Sides ranch went no better. The sheriff's forty-man posse arrived to find that Sides, a tall, heavy man known for his dangerous temper, had rallied an equal number of men, ready with guns and ensconced behind fortifications. The posse rebelled against the sheriff and went home without firing a shot.[27]

One of Orson Hyde's last letters to Brigham Young a few days later reported:

> The old citizens, that is a portion of them have become highly mobocratic. They are going to regulate all matters. They are going to lynch the assessor and collector till he pays back any taxes that he may have collected and cost that have been paid in any law case must be refunded. No man that is a Mormon can live who has more than one wife, every thing must be regulated; and to this end they are said to be enlisting the Indians. . . . There is now no chance for us but victory or death.

Because the attempt to seize his sawmill that Hyde feared did not transpire, no need arose to choose between these apocalyptic alternatives, but it was becoming increasingly clear that decisions made under Utah law could not be enforced because the settlers would not accept them.[28]

Many had admired the ability of the Mormons to develop inhospitable lands in Utah. Pious and industrious, they laid out neat towns, started school systems, and plowed flourishing ranches, rich with stock and crops. Yet American public opinion, especially in the Northeast, was overwhelmingly hostile to the Mormons, and many of the settlers who lived side by side with them apparently shared these attitudes. Mormons rubbed other Americans the wrong way for several reasons. Many believed that the Mormons' ultimate aim was political independence, and this offended their patriotism. They credited frightening stories about the Danites, characterizing them as a Mormon secret police who murdered unbelievers. They listened to the tales of horror that percolated through the West of emigrants and enemies of the church murdered and stock stolen by Indians who "spoke good English." They considered polygamy abhorrent, a moral evil to be classed with slavery, and ascribed it to licentiousness. They were annoyed by the Mormon conviction that Mormons possessed the one and only divinely sanctioned truth destined to overwhelm all other beliefs. Finally, their perception of the Mormons as largely a group of illiterate and indigent foreigners (similar to the Irish) awakened their nativist prejudices, a potent political issue in the 1850s when the proportion of immigrants in the American population had climbed steeply. Though the numbers are fuzzy, this image of the church membership had some basis in fact, as an estimated 70 percent had emigrated, mainly from Britain and Scandinavia, as a result of energetic Mormon proselytizing in Europe in hard times (one of the reasons that Mormons did not go the way of several other American religions that sprang up in the nineteenth century). A plethora of books with such titles as *The Mormons; or, Knavery Exposed, A Narrative of the Experiences of Joseph H. Jackson in Nauvoo, Exposing the Depths of Mormon Villainy,* and *Life in Utah; or, The Mysteries and Crimes of Mormonism: Being an Expose of the Secret Rites and Ceremonies of the Latter-Day Saints, with a Full and Authentic History of Polygamy from Its Origin to the Present Time,* often written by angry apostates, served to fan the flames.[29]

Aside from the prejudices that stirred public opinion, Mormon historian Leonard Arrington sees the cause of the conflict between the Mormons and others as an essential difference in values: communal for the Mormons, with obedience and submission ranking high among the virtues; individualistic, freewheeling, and exploitative for the settlers. Certainly, the Mormons' communal and hierarchical religious values set them apart in an indigestible unit, and others have argued that the unregenerate dislike they inspired originated in the political contest for control. In *Mormonism: Its Leaders and Designs,* an apostate's scathing and influential polemic, John Hyde wrote: "As a church, they have the extremest right to worship whom and what they please. Rites the most ridiculous and fantastic . . . dogmas the most atrocious and profane; leaders the most bigoted or corrupt; people the most fanatic and suicidal may be tolerated as to religion. But when that religion nerves the arm and grasps the sword of secular power . . . wise men need to hesitate before acceding to its demands." In lectures to large audiences in California, this articulate apostate declared that the Mormon effort to gain political ascendancy lay at the root of the past persecutions they had suffered in the Midwest. Orson Hyde's efforts to "secure" the eastern slope left no doubt that fears of Mormon rule had a basis in fact.[30]

As soon as he received permission from Brigham Young to return to Salt Lake City, Orson Hyde wasted no time. He had long felt that during his mission on the western edge of the Mormon empire his talents had languished unappreciated "under a bushel," although his accomplishments appear prodigious. Perhaps in the late autumn of 1856 when he departed for Utah with his mission complete, leaving the colonists prospering on ranches he had surveyed for them, a state boundary established in Utah's favor, a taste of Utah administration, and a substantial bloc of Mormon voters, Hyde already sensed that he had lost by winning. He called his sojourn on the eastern slope his "darkest and least desirable mission, and the most dull and discouraging prospects that ever presented themselves to me." There is no sign that he ever changed his mind.[31]

5

James Crane Explains It All, 1857

I N JUNE 1858 the *Mountain Democrat* in Placerville, California, opined that the creation of a new territory on the eastern slope would "open a fine field for broken down politicians, land grabbers, and office hunters." In fact, the influx had started earlier, and one of the newcomers that many earlier settlers believed fitted this description was Major William Ormsby, Pennsylvania born, then about forty-three, and acquiring his title as major from the state militia. He soon saw possibilities in the West. In 1844 at age thirty, he married sixteen-year-old Margaret Trumbo in Sharpsburg, Kentucky, where he ran a distillery and a gristmill and sold dry goods. Then came the life-transforming event—the California gold rush. In 1849 Ormsby left for California with two brothers and two brothers-in-law, packing overland with mules. Joining his older brother John in California, he pursued a variety of occupations: a private mint in Sacramento, a horse market, a stage line from Sacramento to Coloma, and another to Marysville on the Feather River north of Sacramento. (Once such a man was called a "jack-of-all-trades," but now the preferred terminology is a "flexible frontier capitalist.") When he brought his wife and daughter, Lizzie, to California from Kentucky in 1852, he had obviously decided that their future lay in the West—if not in Central America.[1]

Ormsby's later investments suggest that he had done fairly well, but, like so many forty-niners, he had not gained the fortune of his imagining. In 1856 he reportedly joined the Walker expedition to Ni-

[66]

caragua. The vainglorious William Walker, mad with ambition and attracting many like-minded men, intended to make himself an emperor, seize lands in Nicaragua, sell them to his followers, and ultimately admit several South American countries to the Union as slave states. This adventure (or misadventure) brought Ormsby in contact with another Walker follower, the son of an important Virginia politician, William Smith, who would later play a preliminary role in creating the territory of Nevada.[2]

After Walker's fantastical expedition fizzled, Ormsby sought greener pastures for his ambitions and moved to Genoa in the spring of 1857. His most significant and lasting act there was one that he would scarcely have noticed amid the political maneuverings and land acquisitions that engaged his attention. He took two Paiute girls, daughters of Chief Winnemucca, into his home, probably to learn English in exchange for help with household tasks. It was during a few months at the Ormsbys, under the supervision of Margaret Ormsby, that Sarah Winnemucca acquired the fluency in English and the knowledge of the white world that would one day make her the spokeswoman of the Paiutes and the most influential woman Indian leader of her day, far eclipsing the ambitious man she served. Sarah's presence in the household signified a temporary rapprochement between Ormsby and the Paiutes. She looked on in shock when Ormsby called upon the Paiutes to bring in Washo blamed (evidently in error) for murders in the Sierra Nevada of two pack train operators, John McMarlin and James Williams.[3]

Another notable 1857 arrival was James M. Crane, a friend of Ormsby. Crane was born about 1819 in Richmond, Virginia, which may have been the most significant fact about him. He became a printer of the Whig persuasion, hitching his wagon to a political party soon to disappear and from 1846 to 1848 edited a Virginia newspaper titled the *Southerner.* Although commonly called "Judge Crane," no evidence has emerged that he was ever a judge (he may have simply appropriated the title). His proud claim to be an "old pioneer" was, however, entirely

An ambitious newcomer, William Ormsby.
Courtesy Nevada State Museum, Carson City.

true and remained a source of great satisfaction to him. Already in
1848 the tax assessor found him in San Francisco with two printing
presses. Apparently, he made a brief visit to the East, returning to San
Francisco by ship from Panama in 1852. Here he coedited the *California Courier,* a Whig newspaper that died along with the Whigs, hastened on its way by four fires in its offices and the loss of government
printing contracts.[4]

After the demise of the *Courier,* Crane supported himself as an occasional correspondent for other newspapers and a lecturer. He did
not shrink from vast subjects. Responding to an invitation for a San
Francisco lecture in 1857, he declared he would hold forth upon "the
earth's surface, as known to the ancients from the time of Moses to the
travels of Marco Polo." A second disquisition would cover the mari-

time discoveries of Columbus, da Gama, Magellan, Cook, and others. In future he promised that he would be prepared to speak on the past, present, and future of the islands and continents of the Pacific and Indian Oceans. Nonetheless, his preferred subject was a lengthy and sarcastic oration on discrimination by the U.S. government against California. So unpopular did these lectures prove that Crane eventually renounced the podium: "The mass of the people seem to prefer the hoedowns, fandangoes, wizard and monkey shows, horse operas &c, to anything that might enlighten them about the country." He pursued his own enlightenment by immersing himself in the study of Spanish records and became convinced that the Mexican mineral belts continued in the Great Basin well before any important mineral discovery supported the idea. Given Crane's genuine enthusiasm over future bonanzas in the region, Ormsby may not have had too much difficulty in persuading his friend to join him on the eastern slope. Still, where the settlers' hopes for territorial status were concerned, the most significant fact about Crane was that he was a Virginian—and so was the influential Washington politician William Smith.[5]

Although direct evidence has not yet emerged on the connections among these three men—Crane, Ormsby, and Smith—their paths are so tightly interwoven and their filibustering ideas so compatible that it is difficult to believe that they did not know each other, perhaps rather well. Ormsby and Smith's son James Caleb had gone adventuring with Walker, and James Caleb had died in Nicaragua. William Smith had temporarily deserted Virginia for California, where his political ambitions were thwarted. It nonetheless seems likely that he met the editor of the *California Courier* in the course of his politicking, if he had not already known Crane in Virginia. Smith returned to Virginia and soon to the House Committee on Territories. Crane may have encouraged him to expect that Nevada could become another slave state, but he also had a personal reason for interest in a Nevada territory. Austin E. Smith, another of his sons and a naval officer at the port of San Francisco, had been mentioned as a possible governor for Nevada Territory.[6]

From the ferment in which the West was taking shape out of the chaos, another idea had bubbled to the surface. In the 1850s the concept of a Pacific republic, a separate country comprising California, the Northwest, and the Southwest, enjoyed considerable currency among prominent westerners, and the suspicion arises that Crane may have embraced it. At that time the idea sounded less treasonable than it does to modern ears. Jefferson had envisaged the Far West as American communities, too distant to be within the United States. Others since his time had advocated similar ideas, perhaps several countries to be carved out of the West, sister nations settled by Americans and closely allied to the United States but not within it. The example of Texas gave impetus to this idea, as Texas had been a separate republic before joining the United States. Grievances against the government in Washington, about which Crane inveighed early and late, and the delay in granting statehood to Oregon kept the idea alive. Leading politicians in California and Oregon and several important newspapers advocated it. But, in his book at least, Crane delicately skirted the issue.[7]

In *The Past, the Present and the Future of the Pacific,* a compilation in book form of two of his lectures, Crane called the U.S. government "our most bitter enemy" and railed long and loud against Washington's maltreatment of California. The "old rats" and "spavin-legged nags" in Washington had dispatched boatloads of "worthless loafers" to displace worthy California pioneers in federal offices. Washington had overcharged Californians for postage, mishandled the mail steamer contract, bullied Californians over land titles, attempted to plunder California mineral lands, and, worst of all, failed to construct a transcontinental railroad and a telegraph line to link the West and East Coasts. Crane peppered his exposition of the national government's offenses with dark threats. On the railroad and telegraph issue, he declared that the government "pandering to a few New York capitalists" may force us to "take leave of the Atlantic States forever," while adding that he hoped that day would never come. He warned that if Washington continued to treat the pioneers as Britain did the American colonies they might rebel, words of defiance that paralleled the avowal made at the settlers' meeting in 1851 to take action "as our fathers did" unless freed from Utah's rule.[8]

Despite these menacing rumblings, the vision Crane finally painted was not of a Pacific republic but of a large and influential bloc of western states. Three states would be created from Washington and Oregon, three from California, and three from Utah and part of New Mexico. Sonora and Baja California "will as naturally fall into our hands, as the ripe pear falls to the ground," adding three more states. These twelve western states would send twenty-four senators and thirty-two representatives to Congress. Crane, ever dreamy and imaginative, then waxed lyrical:

> I can see new temples dedicated to Almighty God occupying the places of those where formerly stood temples dedicated to wood and stone. I can see the public school house rising on those spots now consecrated to the war-dance and the funeral pyre. . . . I can hear, upon each returning Fourth of July, the military bands playing the martial airs of this Land of the Free, for a people whose bosoms are swelling with pride and delight. I can behold new countries, inhabited by a free, patriotic, enlightened and energetic people, over which proudly floats the stars and stripes of the Union. . . . The child is even now born, who may behold these wondrous and glorious events.

Crane closed his book with the avowal that he had made the West his permanent home: "Here will I die, and here shall my body be buried." So he would, and sooner than he knew.[9]

When the settlers again gathered on August 8, 1857, Ormsby and Crane assumed leading roles, despite the fact that Ormsby had resided on the eastern slope a scant four months and Crane for only one—the original carpetbaggers. Sudden changes of venue seem to have been generally accepted among frontier people, and Crane apparently saw no parallels between himself and the newly arrived office seekers he had condemned in California—perhaps he thought the credentials of an "old pioneer" were valid anywhere in the West. At a previous meeting a few days earlier, convened by a man walking around with a cowbell, John Reese had been elected president, but on the eighth it was Ormsby who called the Genoa meeting in Gilbert's Saloon to order. While a committee prepared the resolutions to be presented to Washington, Crane gave the assemblage a taste of his oratory by speaking for an hour. Because he could talk at great length, boring his listeners to stupefaction, they recognized him for a real politician, fully qualified to take his place with others of the same breed. The Mormon leader who had also been invited to address the settlers boycotted the meeting.[10]

The resolutions adopted by the meeting commenced with the selection of Crane as the delegate to represent the eastern slope in Washington, D.C., and went on to marshal the arguments for territorial status, some valid and some wild exaggerations. Isolation was their strongest theme. Because many miles and winter snows separated the eastern slope from Utah, California, and the Northwest for much of the year, they were compelled to struggle without government:

> From our anomalous condition during all seasons of the year, no debts can be collected by law; no offenders can be arrested, and no crime can be punished except by the code of Judge Lynch, and no obedience to government can be enforced, and for these reasons there is and can be no protection to either life or property except that which may be derived from the peaceably disposed, the good sense and patriotism of the people, or from the fearful, unsatisfactory, and terrible defense and protection which the revolver, the bowie-knife, and other deadly weapons may afford us.

They rejected the theocratic government of Utah and proposed a huge territory extending from Oregon to Sonora in the grand tradition of Brigham Young's Deseret.[11]

Then came the wild exaggerations. The white population of the eastern slope magically soared from the hundreds to seven or eight thousand. The settlers anticipated an approaching population influx on the scale of the California gold rush that would result in "scenes of a tragical character" unless Congress established a territorial government for them. They also claimed to inhabit 200 to 250 alluvial valleys, "the best *grazing and agricultural lands on this continent*," a remarkably optimistic description of a desert country where agriculture would forever remain limited. They further declared that their own settlements in these numerous rich alluvial valleys and the emigrant trails crossing Nevada needed the protection of a territorial government from the depredations of seventy-five thousand to one hundred thousand hostile Indians (twelve thousand, at most, would have been a more realistic figure). In view of congressional ignorance of the West, these preposterous claims may have slipped by without question. Whatever the validity of their arguments, the settlers had continued to press for territorial status. The history of the nineteenth century would show that communities that allowed their cause to languish often failed to reach the goal for many years. Repeated agitation was critical to success.[12]

Crane had his office. His means of support was another matter. The meeting had resolved that "it is our duty to raise the necessary funds to provide for his expenses." Crane, no doubt for good reason, had little faith that support would be forthcoming and immediately began dunning his constituents. Stephen Kinsey, the Genoa postmaster and an early settler who claimed to have come into the country with Reese in 1851, recalled:

> The want of money obliged him to receive donations to defray his expenses. . . . A few days before his departure, he took me one side, and said he wanted to have a talk. Said he: "Now Kinsey, I cannot promise what I will do for you when I get to Washington and succeed in getting

this Territory organized; but this much I will venture to say: you shall have an office that you will be well satisfied with." This I paid no attention to, as I considered from whence it came. He then requested me to let him have a few dollars, to help him along. I told him I did not believe he could do anything for himself, let alone others, and he need not expect a single dollar from me.

Crane would see to it that Kinsey lost his office, but the durable Kinsey would soon reemerge as deputy recorder.[13]

Picking up endorsements for a territory along the way from California governor John Welles and many California newspapers, Crane soon started on his journey to Washington, where his Virginia connections would serve him well. *San Francisco Herald* correspondent Richard Allen, also known as "Tennessee" and no friend of Crane, later disparagingly suggested that Crane had been dispatched to Washington in order to get rid of him. Ormsby remained on the eastern slope, immersing himself in local politics and accumulating landholdings in Gold Canyon, where he anticipated more mining; Eagle Valley, a likely spot for a future state capital; and other sites. The more he dominated politically and financially, the more his aggressive ambitions aroused resentment among the scattering of old settlers. Factions formed, as commonly occurred in chaotic areas of the frontier lacking the authority of a strong governor. One coalesced around Ormsby and Richard Sides and became known by the ominous name of the Vigilance Committee, probably an attempt to gain legitimacy through a name associated with the highly regarded San Francisco vigilance committees of 1851 and 1856; the other faction surrounded Lucky Bill and his friend Uncle Billy Rogers, the old ex-sheriff from California, and was called the Mormons. As the old settlers in this group were not Mormon, the label seems to have been inherited from the Mormons who had formerly opposed Richard Sides.[14]

During a ball celebrating the opening of Lucky Bill's new White Hotel in Genoa, the hostility between the two factions erupted into a "muss." While the ladies and their escorts danced in the second-floor ballroom, Sides on the first floor endeavored to pick a quarrel with Uncle Billy by making nasty remarks about Lucky Bill and his mistress, Martha Lamb. Uncle Billy, though much older than the large, muscular young Richard Sides, stood his ground. The quarrel evidently grew loud and serious enough to cause a stampede of frightened ladies from the ballroom. It was not an auspicious opening for Lucky Bill's new hotel.[15]

As the two factions faced off in Genoa, much more serious trouble brewed in Utah. For weeks, rumors that the Mormons would soon be recalled to Utah had raced from cabin to cabin, and a wagon train of California Mormons headed for Salt Lake City had already passed through in July. This time the quarrel was no frontier brawl but a confrontation between Brigham Young and the U.S. government. The emotional frenzy of a reformation had seized the Mormons, apparently aroused by the spread of apostasy, and federal officials became targets. Several factors combined to lead President James Buchanan and hotheads in Congress to conclude that the Mormons were in a state of rebellion. Judges, surveyor David H. Burr, and Indian agent Garland Hurt, among others, had fled Utah in fear for their lives, and a mob had broken into Judge Stiles's court to steal federal court records. The Mormons denigrated the judges and the others as "runaway officials" and launched a campaign of character assassination against them. Although there may have been justification in some of their charges—the caliber of federal officials in the West was hardly stellar—those the Mormons rejected probably sank no lower than the political hacks in other western states and territories. The truth was that the Mormons would prefer to be governed by Mormons, and the government would prefer to establish a skeleton crew of federal authorities.[16]

The confrontation developed against a background of damning reports to Washington from the fugitive officials, a vituperative barrage of publications from apostates (including Joseph Smith's own younger brother), and public opinion opposed to the Mormons, denounced in the Senate by Stephen Douglas as "a pestiferous disgusting cancer . . .

[75]

alien enemies and outlaws engaging in treasonable, disgusting and bestial practices." All this the Mormon delegate to Congress, Dr. John Bernhisel, and their advocate, Thomas Kane, strove mightily to counteract, but the tide was gathering force. The 1856 Republican Party platform had sounded the trumpet call for an end to the "twin relics of barbarism: slavery and polygamy."[17]

Buchanan evidently concluded that, in view of the breakdown of federal authority in Utah, the "path of duty" demanded a military escort to install a new territorial governor in place of Brigham Young. In his explanation to Congress, the president cited several reasons for action: Young had been stockpiling weapons, inciting Indian hostility to the United States, and driving out federal officials. Buchanan may also have had political considerations in mind. In view of the deepening sectional split over slavery, a signal that defiance against the authority of the U.S. government would be firmly quashed may have been in order. Further, there is some suspicion that Buchanan, a Democrat with southern sympathies, sought to defuse the furor over slavery by a popular military action against the Mormons.[18]

As a result, one-sixth of the U.S. Army under General William Harney began marching west in midsummer 1857, much too late to reach Salt Lake City before the snows fell in the Rockies, and Brigham Young's resistance began with burning the army's supplies at their encampment on the Green River. The president had erroneously expected the Mormons to offer no resistance, indeed to welcome the army as liberators from ecclesiastical despotism. He could hardly have been more wrong. Both sides, however, refrained from the irrevocable step of engaging in direct battle.[19]

The Mormons Depart, the Groshes Return, 1857

O N AUGUST 17, 1857, Peter Conover, a farmer of forty-nine years, began riding west from Utah on an urgent errand for Brigham Young. He traveled with several other men and a guide, present because to speed the journey the party had been instructed to diverge from the well-worn emigrant trail on a more direct route. It proved to be an unwise decision. Indeed, Brigham Young's riders would have benefited from the advice of Virginia Reed, a survivor of the Donner party: "Don't take no cutoffs." Time and again, the guide led the thirsty men and animals to a promised source of water that had gone dry. At one point, they traveled twenty-four hours without food, drink, or rest, "almost perishing with thirst and hunger." Conover's tongue became so badly swollen that he could scarcely keep it in his mouth. The guide appeared lost. In Conover's words: "The guide had completely given up. He could neither see, hear or make a sound. He had given up to die and had told one of the boys what to do with everything that he had and what message to give his wife and friends at home." When the party at last reached a "blessed haven" of water, they guzzled it recklessly and threw it over each other.[1]

On the morning of September 1, they reached the Washoe Valley settlement where Judge Chester Loveland lived and delivered Brigham Young's message. Countermanding his recent letter assuring the colony that he was not recalling them from their mission, Young directed them to "rally back to Salt Lake City" to defend the faith against the advancing U.S. Army and to raise as much money as possible to buy arms and ammunition in California. At meetings Loveland immediately called in Washoe, Eagle, and Carson Valleys, all available funds were collected and entrusted to a clerk who made regular trips to California for merchandise and could buy the ammunition on the sly.[2]

Bringing this valuable shipment safely to Salt Lake City required subterfuge and liberal amounts of whiskey, especially after the *Sacramento Bee* broke the story, arousing the patriotic fervor of miners who gathered at the tavern in Angels Camp where Conover awaited delivery. Although his religion forbade spirituous beverages, Conover had prudently laid in a supply of whiskey, and as soon as the wagon containing ammunition arrived, he locked it in the warehouse. He then opened a keg for the miners and, while they swilled it, unloaded the gunpowder (unrecognized in boxes) with the regular merchandise. By the time the miners turned their attention to ammunition, none remained. Smaller wagons containing the powder started across the Sierra Nevada around midnight. The next morning Conover and two companions followed with the main wagon. Though they had found nothing, the miners remained suspicious. Their leader declared his intention to follow them, and Conover, in his turn, threatened to "bury you without a sheet."[3]

Obedient to the orders of their leaders, the Mormons on the eastern slope hastily prepared for departure, leaving crops unharvested, fledgling orchards they would never tend, a new threshing machine bought with pride, and much else. Some regrets darkened their preparations. Abraham Hunsaker had expected to reap a "bounteous harvest" at "the best farm I ever owned in my life." In his autobiography, Richard Bentley wrote that the order to depart "filled the Saints with consternation, as we had all become comfortably settled, and were being prospered." Yet, excepting a handful of apostates, leave they did on September 26, 450 faithful Mormons in a long train of 123 wagons. During their thirty-seven-day journey, three infants died and six were born. The California miners did pursue them into the desert as threatened, but by posting a strong guard and distributing more whiskey, Conover prevented them from stampeding the horses. The neighbors of the departing Mormons watched their fidelity to their faith with grudging admiration even as they seized the opportunity to take over Mormon lands for little or nothing.[4]

While these wagons rumbled slowly across the desert, rumors of an unimaginable atrocity in southern Utah on September 11 began to circulate. One hundred twenty corpses, men, women, and children, stripped of clothing and jewelry, lay festering in the sun at Mountain Meadows. The Fancher wagon train of California-bound emigrants from Arkansas, an unusually wealthy party with valuable goods and one thousand head of stock, had been surrounded by local Mormon settlers and a number of Indian allies in a siege of several days. The Mormons promised to lead the men to safety if they would lay down their arms—then shot them all. Disguised as Indians, the Mormons then massacred the women and children. Only children under seven were spared in the belief that they were too small to tell what they had seen. Yet one day some of these children would speak, pointing out the murderers and the Mormon women wearing clothes and jewelry that had belonged to their slain mothers.[5]

As is often true of atrocities, any possible explanation seems inadequate, in the words of Mormon church historian Richard Turley, "incongruous with the people who did it." Whether Brigham Young ordered the butchery remains a matter of debate, but recent studies argue persuasively that nothing happened in Utah without Young's "direct orders," that he may have wished to demonstrate his control over the western trails and the Indians to the advancing U.S. Army, and that he may have sought revenge for the recent murder of Mormon apostle Parley Pratt in Arkansas. In the words of Will Bagley's definitive history, *Blood of the Prophets: Brigham Young and the Massacre at Mountain Meadows*, "the Lord's anointed inspired, executed, and covered up a mass murder."[6]

Without doubt, conditions were volatile in southern Utah, where

The Mountain Meadows Massacre. From T. B. H. Stenhouse, *The Rocky Mountain Saints: A Full and Complete History of the Mormons, from the First Vision of Joseph Smith to the Last Courtship of Brigham Young,* facing p. 426. Courtesy Nevada Historical Society, Reno.

war fever had maddened local settlers led by John D. Lee. After all, this was a time when a traveler wrote in his journal of his enforced attendance at a Mormon camp of two or three hundred men, where the evening prayer besought the destruction of the U.S. Army and the torture of all Gentiles. Moreover, poverty may have pressed those in southern Utah to rob and kill in order to acquire the possessions of the Fancher party, and the need of supplies for the war effort may have eased their consciences. Afterward, Lee and the Indians paraded about displaying their plunder. Twenty years later Lee would be executed, in his own eyes a scapegoat, and indisputably the only one among many to be held accountable.[7]

Whether Brigham Young had given the fatal order or not, his fiery words certainly inflamed the war fever that played so large a part in the murders of the emigrants. He proclaimed that the army had been sent to destroy the Mormons and imposed martial law. He would "cut the thread" and declare his kingdom independent. He pronounced that the "mob"—a term for the U.S. Army that aroused emotional memories of past Mormons sufferings at the hands of mobs—must not enter Utah. In a September 14 letter to one of his subordinates, he wrote: "We intend to desolate the Territory and conceal our families, Stock, and all our effects in the fastnesses of the mountains, where they will be safe while the men, waylay our enemies, attack them from ambush, stampede their animals, take the Supply trains cut off detachments . . . to lay waste to everything that will burn, houses, fences, trees, fields, grass, that they cannot find a particle of any thing that will be of use to them, not even sticks to make a fire for to cook their suppers." Soon, in a shift in tactics from belligerence to withdrawal, he decided on the "move south," by which his people would depart for the oases of southern Utah. In all this warmongering, the settlers of the eastern slope, an unwilling attachment to Young's kingdom, had no say whatsoever, and as they heard of the horror at Mountain Meadows their desire to be free of Utah undoubtedly intensified.[8]

And hear they surely did, along with the entire West and the nation. In the words of the *San Francisco Bulletin,* "the blood of American citizens cries for vengeance." The Mormons made every effort to blame the mass murder upon the Indians, if it could not be entirely concealed. When Young made his report to the government more than a year later, he ascribed the event to Indian revenge. The settlers responsible took an oath that the name of no white man at the scene of the crime would ever be revealed. After the courageous federal judge John Cradlebaugh subsequently conducted an investigation and issued thirty-six writs, all those named evaded arrest. A woman schoolteacher who asked too many questions was shot and killed (her murderer was never tried). Mormon guides led emigrant parties passing through southern Utah along routes that avoided the scene of the massacre. Yet blood would speak. The Mormons, some appalled by what had happened at Mountain Meadows, talked among themselves, travelers carried stories, and, as Mormon historian Juanita Brooks wrote, "the word spread like wildfire," reaching the eastern press within two months. Angry public meetings convened in California.[9]

The fate of the Fancher party appeared to confirm past allegations of Mormon murders of travelers and apostates, as well as the belief that the Mormons incited Indians to violence and disguised themselves as Indians to commit crimes. Moreover, the stigma lasted for years and seriously damaged the Mormon bid for statehood. In 1859 Hannah Clapp, a fierce and determined woman who attended Salt Lake City Mormon services in bloomers packing a revolver and later became well known as a pioneer teacher on the eastern slope, visited the survivor children and heaped scorn upon the Mormons: "Oh! I know we are in a foreign land; not American soil here! This is the 'Independent State of Deseret.'" Mark Twain remembered the massacre long afterward: "The whole United States rang with its horrors." The petitioners on the eastern slope may well have hoped that this widespread execration of all things Mormon might lend an added boost to their hopes for separation. And, being traders, they hoped for added revenues if U.S. troops and supplies were shipped east from California for the coming war with the Mormons.[10]

The year 1857 was a time of restless discontent for California miners. No longer could a prospector pan the streams for a good living while hoping for a great bonanza. The surface had been picked over, and mining had become an industrial enterprise requiring considerable capital to extract deeper gold deposits. Unwilling to abandon the old way of life for industrial employment, prospectors had dashed off hopefully to the excitements at the Kern River in the southern Sierra

Nevada, east of present-day Bakersfield, in 1855 and Canada's Fraser River three years later only to be disappointed. The Kern River had little gold, and the Fraser River deposits, though rich, were difficult to work. Few suspected that the next great bonanza lay just over the Sierra Nevada because, in the phrase of author Charles Shinn, the eastern slope appeared to be a "played-out country." Many traders had folded their tents with the steep decline in emigrant traffic; the Mormons had departed, a loss to the development of agriculture; and the Gold Canyon placers had been "cleaned up to bed rock" several times over. Estimated gold production sank to the lowest point since the first year when prospectors began shaking their pans and shoveling gravel into their Long Toms, a mere $18,200. Even the winter snows failed, and little snowmelt trickled into the ravine to sluice their rockers. Of nearly two hundred miners working the canyon in the peak year, 1854, probably no more than twenty-five remained. Although the available estimates do not provide a definitive count, the white population on the eastern slope may have sunk below six hundred. Nonetheless, though the buoyant spirits of their early days in California had evaporated, the Grosh brothers kept the faith.[11]

For prospectors who thought they had found black silver ore "in masses as large as your fist," Allen and Hosea showed remarkable restraint. Excepting a brief return trip in 1856, they absented themselves from Gold Canyon until the spring of 1857. The reasons that emerge in their letters to their father are several. Despite their initial optimism, they had second thoughts on the value of their discovery because they had not tested the ore ("We may be mistaken"). Also, and not for the first time, they were distracted. In the spring of 1856, they began work on the last and most fanciful of their marvelous inventions, a perpetual-motion machine. As with their previous ventures in mechanics, their hopes soared ("There can be no question as to our success. It will work"). If this was not distraction enough, they threw themselves heartily into the presidential campaign of John Charles Frémont, one of the nineteenth century's most talented *spinmeisters*. Frémont had turned his court-martial for mutiny and other charges stemming from his activities in California into a public relations triumph featuring himself and emerged nearly ten years later as the first presidential candidate of the newly forming Republican Party in 1856. The campaign slogan, "Free Soil, Free Men, Frémont, and Victory," aroused all the boyish enthusiasm of the Groshes, who were never neutral about anyone or anything, and they shortened their mid-September Gold Canyon trip to only a few weeks in order to canvass the California gold country for him ("We have done considerable in spreading light on the subject").[12]

Nonetheless, the main reason for their long delay in returning to Gold Canyon seems to have been poverty. The brothers believed they needed a stake of perhaps $200 to buy equipment and to support themselves while they tested the ore and prospected the area. Otherwise, they would need to placer gold in order to live, with no time to pursue silver. In a despairing mood they wrote to their father: "O this bitter poverty! For three years now we have been steeped in it to the very lips. Nothing prospers in our hands—yet we are patient and industrious. We sometimes think that Providence keeps us back until our time ... come—else why this unaccountable, never ending streack of bad luck? For this past two years we have been too poor to get out of mining, but have been driven on like arastir [arrastra] horses, blindfolded."[13]

Finally, in November 1856, they sold their California claim for $150, took in a partner, and expressed their intention to winter in Gold Canyon. Their brief visit had shown the need for a speedy return. The landmarks they erected had been destroyed; with other prospectors in the area, a claim would not wait indefinitely. Yet they did not go. Evidently, a healthy respect for the dangers of travel through the winter snows of the high Sierra Nevada changed their minds. It is unfortunate that Allen would not always exhibit similar prudence.[14]

In late May 1857 they at last returned to Gold Canyon and by midsummer were hard at work assaying: "We cupelled with a hand bel-

lows, by piling charcoal over the cupell Unfortunately the antimony
. . . caused the lead to scatter & divide into little globules thro' the slag
and we tried to gather them together with borax, in which we only
partially succeeded. . . . Day after day & week after week we were at it
from daylight to dark, hanging over glowing furnaces, and the ther-
mometer in the 'nineties.'" Nor had they abandoned their efforts to
devise the perpetual-motion machine. They were somewhat surprised
to find Gold Canyon "mad with the Prospecting fever"—a momentary
blip in the prevailing doldrums. Apparently, their stake proved in-
sufficient, and they needed to fall back on placering for a living once
more. When they completed their tests on the silver ore and their in-
vestigations of the terrain, they expected to receive development capital from George Brown, a trader at the Humboldt Sink who had kept
an eye on their claims during their absence. They had already formed
a mining company in which their friends and relatives held a stake,
and the old dream of a family colony in the West blossomed again.
They saw the population of the eastern slope as the "refuse of California & Mormons." But, led by the Grosh clan, a "great race" could spring
up, fired by "free impulsive energy."[15]

They held the existing population in contempt: "The old settlers of
Carson instead of tending to their farms are principally engaged in
trading (i.e., robbing) with the emigrants to Cal. when there are any.
When there is no emigration they rob each other." They gave the Mormons credit for industrious farming and wrote their father an analysis
of Mormon law, of which, being Groshes, they had obviously made a
thorough study. They saw "polygama" as the "corner stone of Mormonism—on it is reared the whole superstructure—and of its practical
working you can hardly believe to much if you believe the very worst
stories in circulation." The brothers strongly condemned Mormon
rule:

> The object of the elders is clear. Their aim is to build up an aristocracy
> as strong & pedious as the oligarchy of our Southern states. By appro-
> priating to themselves "exclusive control" of water privileges & valuable

woodland "regulating" the "use" of the first & the "roads" through the last, receiving fees & collecting tolls thereon they have made great strids towards making permanent their power. Their "wives" are nothing more than slaves.

Yet, despite their recent political activity in California, Allen and Hosea took no part in the settlers' efforts to escape Mormon dominance by forming a new territory.[16]

In mid-August tragedies far beyond hardship and failure overwhelmed them. The lesser was the murder at Gravely Ford of their backer, George Brown, by Arkansas travelers after Indians killed several head of their stock. Brown's detractors claimed that he had been trading guns to Indians, who paid for them by stealing emigrant stock. The Groshes hotly disputed such calumnies against "one of the few right good men in Utah." They wrote their father that Brown, "a shoemaker by trade, fond of traveling & a great wanderer," was a fortyniner who had lived on the eastern slope since 1853: "In a community no way distinguished for virtue, he stood like Paul in the congregation of Israel, and all bore testimony to his worth & integrity." Whatever the truth about Brown—gunrunner amassing illegal profits or pillar of virtue—the Groshes had lost their only source of investment.[17]

The greater tragedy, however, was the gash Hosea accidentally cut in his foot with a pick. At first the brothers made light of it, expecting that Hosea would be bedridden for no more than three or four weeks while the wound healed. Allen applied poultices of rosin soap for a week, and Hosea seemed to improve. But on the eighth day the foot swelled and the wound closed. Allen lanced the foot and tried a bread and soda poultice, then switched to Indian meal. The foot became very painful, strange sensations began, and fever set in. Nonetheless, Hosea made light of his sufferings in an effort to allay his brother's fears. A friend at the store where Allen traveled to get opium recommended an old pioneer remedy, a fresh cow dung poultice, which Allen hopefully applied. The foot began turning cold. Leaving Hosea in the care of their partner, William ("Cap") Galphin, Allen set off on foot, cutting across the hills on a rough trail, to consult a doctor in Eagle Valley. Dr. King advised continuing the cow dung poultices and assured Allen that none of the symptoms he reported were worrisome.[18]

The doctor was wrong. By the time Allen reached their cabin at dark on September 2, Hosea had died of blood poisoning. Galphin reported that he had died peacefully in his sleep. Allen was stricken: "Oh the terrible force of that blow! Oh! the utter desolation of that hour!" His deep religious faith shone through in the letter he wrote to their father:

> I take up my pen with a heavy heart, for I have sad news to send you. God has seen fit in his perfect wisdom & goodness to call Hosea, the patient, the good, the gentle. . . . In the first burst of my sorrow, I complained bitterly of the dispensation which deprived me of what I held most dear of all the world, and I thought it most hard that he should be called away, just as we had fair hopes of realizing what we had labored for so hard for so many years. But when I reflected how well an upright life had prepared him for the next, and what a debt of gratitude I owed to God in blessing me for so many years with so dear a companion, I became calm, and bowed my head in resignation. Oh Father thy will and not mine be done.[19]

Although tempted to leave the West, Allen decided it was his "duty" to carry on with the mining enterprise on which they had labored so long and hard. He would make further efforts to determine the value of their silver claims, then winter in San Francisco. Unfortunately, he delayed too long. It was November 15 when Allen and a young Canadian named Maurice Bucke finally set off to cross the mountains by a little-traveled route, despite the general understanding that after October the weather in the high Sierra Nevada became too risky. At Washoe Lake they lost another five days hunting for their runaway jack. By the time they reached Squaw Valley, snow had started to fall, and, in Bucke's words, "we were completely caught," unable to turn back. On two successive days, they tried to ascend the remaining

[87]

mountains, but the snow was so deep that they could not see the trail. They were forced back to Squaw Valley. Being out of provisions, they killed their pack animal and "lived on the unfortunate jack the rest of the time."[20]

It was now November 24. While snow continued to fall, they stayed in the Squaw Valley cabin fashioning snowshoes. When they finally started out again on the twenty-ninth, they found they had taken the wrong route and returned to the cabin "nearly frosen and tired out." The next day they succeeded in ascending the summit and reaching a cabin on the other side, only to find that the provisions Bucke expected there had been stolen. Another snowstorm blew in, so they remained in the cabin, with about three days' worth of jack meat. Because their matches had gotten wet, they started a fire with a gun. Although snow continued to fall, they set out again, following the American River and burying themselves in the snow at night to keep from freezing. After they climbed a rocky ridge with great difficulty and found no human habitation, Bucke said to Allen that "we might as well lay there until we died." But Allen had not yet lost heart. He responded that "as long as he could crawl he would not give up."[21]

Exhausted, cold, and starving, they would soon be reduced to crawling through the snow. At last they came to a ditch and followed it to a miner's cabin where they were tenderly cared for. According to Bucke, they had been seventeen days in the snowbound mountains. As neither could walk on their frozen feet, miners brought them down on sleighs to Last Chance, where an Italian family cared for them so kindly that Allen felt "the only trouble we find is to prevent them doing to much for us." Although Allen's feet had frozen to the knees, he thought the blanket wrappings, liniment, and poultices applied to them had been more effective than Bucke's method of warming his feet by the fire, and he optimistically expected to be up and around in a few days. By the time the doctor the miners had sent for arrived from Michigan Bluff, Allen had developed a high fever. Maurice Bucke survived the amputation of both his frostbitten feet and went on to become the director of a mental hospital in Canada. Allen died on December 19. After the loss of Hosea, Allen had written: "We had lived so much together, with & for each other that I was [of the] earnest desire that we might pass out of the world as we had passed through it—hand in hand." Less than four months after Hosea's death, his earnest desire had come to pass.[22]

The Grosh brothers left behind a grieving family, two mining companies, practically no record of the location of their claims, and a central mystery that still hovers over the Virginia Range: had they discovered the Comstock Lode? Any papers Allen might have brought with him had been lost in the snow. Like most prospectors, the Groshes were secretive about their discoveries. In contrast to other mining districts where records of claims were carefully kept, no record book survives from Gold Canyon in this period, and the brothers nowhere mention recording claims in their detailed descriptions of their activities. Henry Comstock, a slippery and untrustworthy character who would later give his name to the great lode, moved into their stone cabin. The suspicion has been voiced that he appropriated their claims and any records pertaining to them. The Groshes' description of silver in "masses as large as your fist" and a "monster vein" certainly suggests a major discovery, but the principal evidence that it was, in fact, the Comstock comes from Mrs. Laura M. Dettenrieder (Mrs. Ellis in the days when she knew the Groshes). When she stopped by their stone cabin along the trail in American Wash, they gave her an ore sample, told her she was included in the claim they had staked, exhibited the record book in which the claim was transcribed, and showed her where it was located: "We went out upon some elevated ground, and pointing to Mount Davidson, [Allen] said 'It is down at the base of that point.'" That, of course, was the location of the Comstock Lode. Mrs. Dettenrieder added suspiciously, "I should like to know what became of the record book they showed me, that was left in Comstock's possession." One additional source from a Comstocker who knew them well supports discovery by the Groshes. Author Charles

Shinn cites a now lost manuscript by Francis J. Hoover stating that the Groshes posted a claim notice at the axis of the lode on the future lucrative sites of the Ophir and the Gould and Curry Mines.[23]

Dettenrieder's mention of a record book poses a puzzle. The normal practice in a mining district would be election of a recorder who would keep a book in which the claims of all miners in the district were set down. Yet although miners had worked Gold Canyon for a number of years, no such book has come to light. Perhaps the population of the area was too dispersed, fluctuating, and disorganized. It is also possible that the reason can be traced to mobility: because the miners placered, rather than pursuing lode mining, they frequently moved on to a new spot, never settling for long at a fixed location worth recording. Moreover, William Dolman, who arrived in Gold Canyon in mid-November 1857, narrowly missing Allen Grosh, relates that the miners elected him first recorder of what was then known as the Columbia District and he kept the first *Quartz Mining Laws and Records* book east of the Sierra Nevada. It thus seems evident that the book that Allen showed Dettenrieder was a personal account, not an official one.[24]

On the whole, most old Comstockers and historians maintain that the Groshes failed to strike the Comstock Lode. Dolman conversed with Galphin, the friend and partner of the Groshes who had stayed with Hosea on the day he died. As they walked the ground together, Galphin pointed out the deposit the Groshes had been working a mile and a half west from Devil's Gate at the site later known as the Pioneer Lode, not the Comstock. He also related that the brothers had studied metallurgy but lacked practical experience (as their letters confirm); he believed that they doubted to the last that they had found silver. Walking over, Dolman saw evidence of a little mining at the site. The furnace used by the Groshes was also observed on a bench on the slope of the Gold Canyon ravine, not far from their cabin on American Flat. Although the brothers might have ranged widely, these sites all lay south of the main Comstock on what the authoritative historian Grant

H. Smith calls the "Silver City branch of the Comstock Lode," later extensively developed but never profitable, and Galphin, well acquainted with the Groshes and described by Dolman as an honest man that one could "tie to," appears to be a strong witness.[25]

The reputation of the Groshes dived after the mining company they had established was sold. The new owners of the "Grosch Consolidated Gold & Silver Mining Company" commenced litigation in the 1860s to acquire the Ophir and the Gould and Curry mines, flooded the West with propaganda, publicized a false diary, and sold stock. The pamphlet begins by misspelling the Grosh name and erroneously asserting that the brothers made their discovery when pausing at Gold Canyon after crossing the Plains (they had actually traveled to California by way of Mexico). It goes on to cite witnesses (without naming any) and records and diagrams (without reproducing any). Amid further errors and poisonous invective against newspaper editors such as the "imp of infamy" who had not supported them, their case depended upon Henry Comstock, whom they contended had illegally acquired the Grosh claim when he took over their cabin and later sold it. One day Comstock would indeed sell a piece of the lode after others discovered it, but he based his interest on his own claim to ranch land and the water right to a spring, not on a mining claim discovered by the Groshes.[26]

Author Eliot Lord calls the lawsuit "a clear case of black-mail"—one that would undoubtedly have appalled the honest and upright Allen and Hosea. The cases were dismissed, with the defendants' substantial expenses charged to the company. Apart from this episode, the sympathetic public of the day and the historians viewed the Grosh brothers as tragic figures who died on the brink of fortune. Although they had not discovered the great lode, in time they would surely have done so because, in Smith's words, they were "the first in that region to prospect intelligently for silver."[27]

Devils Reign, 1858

I N 1857 a twenty-one-year-old Rhode Island farm boy arrived on the eastern slope. Peleg Brown was not an important man. Indeed, he tried hard not to be important, lest he attract the attention of frontier roughs who might covet his land and stock or ambitious men who might see him as a rival. Nonetheless, the letters he wrote to his family in Rhode Island tell us much about life on the eastern slope as experienced by an ordinary settler who was neither a Mormon apostle, a hardened frontiersman, a gold rush gambler, nor an aspiring politician. Notations indicate that the letters often took a month or more to reach their destination, "dew cours of mail," in Peleg's phrase.

Peleg Brown's letters commence when he was still a schoolboy at a Greenwich boarding school. From the outset, they reveal that spelling was not a subject at which he excelled and that he was restless and disinclined to academic studies ("I am very sory to say that I am sick of staying in this place"). Though obviously a convivial young man devoted to his family and friends, he was also susceptible to the lure of the West, which he represented to his sister Lydia as a business proposition having nothing to do with gold: "I think there is a gred deel better chance for an young man that is just startin in life in some of these western states than at home." His father apparently agreed and gave a substantial loan (with interest) for the undertaking. Letters and census records indicate that Peleg's older brother Joshua had made two earlier trips to California, one in 1851–1852 and the other in 1854–1856. Together with Joshua, Peleg started forth in January 1857 and did a bit of sightseeing on the way, walking up the Capitol steps at Washington, D.C., with his dog, Roam, at his heels. By April they were buying stock in Kentucky. They planned to sell their cattle for a high price in California, telling the family to direct their mail to Sacramento. Then they would return home to Rhode Island as rich men. Simple as that, and the whole venture should take only about a year. In April Peleg wrote that they had not yet "deamed it safe to venture," with a late, cold spring and feed scarce for their herd of 203 cattle. This was not a large herd for the 1850s, which included a band of 10,000 sheep on the California trail.[1]

When they finally deemed it safe to venture, Peleg evidently passed through the waterless deserts and other rigors of the trail without undue difficulty, but the journey left him with an abiding fear and distrust of Mormons. In a letter written soon after his arrival on the eastern slope, he related that two Mormons leading a band of one hundred Indians had extorted $150, horses, and blankets from the wagon train they accompanied on the flimsy pretext that these were needed to make a treaty with the Indians. He also harbored a recurrent fear that the Mormon Avenging Angels, the Danites, might attack and steal his stock. As yet unknown to Peleg, the day he wrote—September 11—was one that justified his apprehensions about Mormons in the bloodiest way. It was the date of the Mountain Meadows Massacre.[2]

They arrived as the Mormons of the eastern slope were preparing to depart and selling their fine ranches for "a mear trifle." This opportunity brought a sudden change of plans. Peleg thought the eastern slope "splendid country for cattle" and found beef prices as high as could be expected in California. When early snows threatened, bringing the herd safely over the mountains that they now saw rising so steeply thousands of feet from the valley floor seemed a perilous proposition. Joshua bought three ranches totaling one thousand acres and a stone house from the Mormons in Washoe Valley for $250 and two more in the Truckee Meadows. He soon departed for the East by sea to bring his wife and children and another herd of stock, while Peleg stayed with the cattle and the ranches, slightly amazed to find himself where he was ("Little did I think . . . that I would ever write to you from Utah"). Although the animals had "started dying quite rapped" at the end of the overland trip, their losses were comparatively small. On acquaintance with the alpine winters in Washoe Valley, Peleg shifted his stock to the milder weather of the Truckee Meadows and later bought a ranch in the Steamboat Springs area (the present Double Diamond Ranch development). He would one day call it "the finest plaice in the valley."[3]

Peleg thought the eastern slope a "barbarous country" but marvelous in many respects. He enjoyed the weather, the warm, sunny winter days in which light snows in the valleys melted quickly while the peaks of the Sierra Nevada shone white all winter—a contrast to the cold and gloom of New England. He often lapsed into pleasant calculations on selling the cattle he had bought at only $15 per head for $50 or $100 and the butter his helpers were churning for 50 cents a pound. The cattle thrived ("All I will have to do to them will be to ride about and see them grow"). And so did Peleg, signing himself, "Your affectionate son in love and prosperity." It amazed him that he had never been sick a day, and he took a certain pride in his western appearance in his new buckskin pants, remarking that cousin George "would think it quite an novelty if he could but sea me here in the mountains and among the savages." Yet he missed books, newspapers, fruit, letters from home (all too rare), and above all "socety," by which he meant the presence of respectable white women. "I am so loathsome at times," he confessed.[4]

Despite his isolation and the lack of newspapers, Peleg seemed well aware of local political developments and interested in them (perhaps he was unconsciously putting down roots). As Washoe Valley dissolved into anarchy, he "tried to get the people together to make some

Peleg Brown in later years when he became a Washoe
County commissioner. Courtesy Benjamin Damonte.

laws," without success. "There is no law here and most of the people
that are here in the valleys are people that don't care for themselves or
anyone else," he observed. He hoped that if territorial status could be
won, lawlessness would end. In the spring he was appointed a delegate
to a meeting that made regulations on landholding and other matters,
but these rules had little effect in the absence of an effective authority
to enforce them.[5]

Law and order were matters of immediate concern to Peleg because
in Joshua's absence he could not hold his brother's Washoe Valley
properties: "One of Joshua ranches has been jumped. . . . I cant get

him off without fighting fort if I set out I can drive him off but we have cattle and he might take revenge out of them." In a letter to Joshua, he explained at greater length:

> I have had considerable trouble about that ranch in Wassau Valley thir has been an man jumped on it he says that he wount move off of it I have tryed to git him off peacible but he wount leave their has been quite an band of lawless fellow moved in the Valley wich . . . the majority of the people are of this kind and the main order of the day is to jump clames whear ever nou one is liveing. . . . All the way is to fight it out if it want for our Cattle I would drive him off wether or no but I think it will bee more mony in out pockits to let him. . . . I cant hold but too clames one in your name, and the other for me Old Mr. Hail offerd me a yearling ster for the clame taking the fighting on his own shoulders the ster is worth about 20 dollars I shall try to do better, but if I cant . . . the ster will probiley will be worth 50 dollars by fall so you wount loose any thing.

The ranch had only cost Joshua $50.[6]

Although he took the precaution of tying his dog, Roam, at the door to prevent theft, Peleg's relations with the Indians appeared friendly. He had an Indian helper for a while, and the Indians sold him fish and deer meat. A Paiute chief (probably Winnemucca) stopped by for a friendly chat on the way to Honey Lake and offered to show Peleg a gold mine if the young man would build him a house, but Peleg showed no interest in mining. Later, when trouble erupted at Honey Lake, the Indians asked him to assure the settlers of their peaceful intentions. Despite warnings from some other settlers that the Indians might be troublesome, Peleg feared Mormons far more than Indians.[7]

Whether Joshua would be safe from the Mormons in crossing the Plains with his family and more stock during the 1858 travel season was a worry that continually preyed on Peleg's mind. He had heard disturbing rumors, true and false: the Mormons had halted all emigration across the Plains; they would plunder and kill all small parties; they had taken the troops prisoner and burned their wagons. "Emigration wount have much show unless protected by Uncle Sams men." In fact, he had no cause for concern because the war that threatened in 1857 had evaporated. Both President Buchanan and Brigham Young had drawn back from their intransigent positions. Under fire in Congress for the expense of dispatching so large a military force in peacetime, Buchanan arrived at the view that an accommodation could be reached and began to entertain peace feelers from Young. For his part, Young had realized that he could not obtain enough arms and ammunition to fight the U.S. Army and that the "move south" was unrealistic because those lands provided scant resources. On April 6, 1858, Buchanan issued a full pardon to the Mormons, which the Mormon leaders accepted on June 12 when they agreed to allow the army to march through Salt Lake City. Both leaders then resorted to face-saving devices. Young settled for a temporary move a short way south; Buchanan established a small military post forty miles south of Salt Lake City at Camp Floyd and installed an innocuous governor, Alfred Cumming, who wielded nominal authority while Young ruled in fact. The return of many Mormons to the eastern slope that Peleg anticipated after the crisis did not come to pass. Nor did the Mormon violence that was never far from his mind, but the lawless condition of the eastern slope continued.[8]

Although the resolution of the Mormon crisis signified a laudable return to good sense in Washington and Salt Lake City, it seriously damaged James Crane's efforts to win territorial status for the eastern slope. The delegate was initially pessimistic, believing Congress too absorbed with "personal schemes and partisan measures" to take an interest in so remote a place. Interest quickened when the looming war with the Mormons enabled Crane to argue that a new territory would "compress the limits of the Mormons" and "defeat their efforts to corrupt and confederate with the Indian tribes." Important assistance came from William ("Extra Billy") Smith, the old acquaintance from Virginia who belonged to the House Committee on Territories and introduced the territorial bill; California senator David Broderick; and the California governor and legislature, which petitioned Congress in January 1858 in favor of the plan. Historian Guy L. Rocha has determined that the first appearance of the name Nevada occurred during the bill's incubation in the House committee and represented the rejection of a variety of other names, including Sierra Nevada. Smith, to whom Crane declared the settlers owed "an everlasting debt of gratitude," may have been moved by hopes for another slave state at the same time that he obliged an old friend, whereas Broderick foresaw lucrative sales to the army via routes originating in northern California.[9]

Crane waxed so optimistic that in a letter of February 18, 1858, to his constituents he urged them to plant heavy crops for sale to the army and the Indians on future reservations. Ever the visionary, he also hoped for mail routes under covered bridges crossing the Sierra Nevada. In April the House received from President Buchanan himself the citizens' memorial requesting a territory—the result of Crane's assiduous lobbying. In May Smith made a vigorous speech in support of the bill, claiming that the Mormons had attacked wagon trains and government mails and darkly warning that if the bill did not pass, the region "would be left in unbroken wilderness, its deep repose broken only by the cry of the wild beast and the yell of the roaming savage." Nonetheless, the times were not propitious for territorial bills. The Compromise of 1850 intended to resolve the divisive issue of the extension of slavery to new western territories broke down in 1854. A prolonged conflict then began over the admission of Kansas and Nebraska as free or slave states against a background of violence in "bleeding Kansas." Long since disenchanted with territorial bills after the bruising Kansas-Nebraska wrangle, Congress reverted to its previous state of disinterest when the threat of hostilities with the Mormons faded, and the territorial bill died in the Committee of the Whole. The "country of ourselves" that Peleg and many other settlers had hoped for was not yet to be.[10]

Joshua, seriously ill in Kansas at Riley City, would not deem it safe to venture in 1858, and Peleg would be obliged to carry on alone—very much alone, for he reported only one other inhabitant in the Truckee Meadows at that time. "I dont know but I shell turn indian, . . ." he wrote. "They are nerely all of the company I have." But Peleg was full of plans. He would have a plow forged by a blacksmith because no manufactured plow could be transported to the eastern slope. He would plant barley and wheat. He might go to Mexico and bring out a band of Mexican horses. He took increasing pleasure in his surroundings: "If there were some kind of socity . . . there would no part of the eastern states which would contain me." In late October, with the miscarriage of his plans, he sank into despair: "I maid a perfect failure." The crops had not matured due to lack of water, a number of cattle had died or been sold to meet a payment, others had mixed with a herd of Spanish cattle grazing freely on the unfenced lands of the Meadows, and he had lost customers when the Fraser River rush emptied Gold Canyon. He came close to selling out for ten thousand dollars, but luckily for his future fortunes the deal fell through. Nonetheless, he was young and resilient, and with the coming of the new year his spirits revived. He could write to Lydia: "I have not been nere as loathsom this winter as last I am getting some what weaned from home."[11]

⚜

Mobs and vigilantes were not the same thing, although mobs often liked to claim that they were vigilantes, compelled to take action when normal government authorities faltered. Vigilantes had a regular organization and remained in existence for some time; mobs, on the other hand, gathered suddenly for a single vengeful act and as suddenly disappeared. Vigilantes, often an economic elite ejecting upstarts, showed a dimension of class warfare that was lacking in heterogeneous mobs. In the wake of the tradition of vigilance committees in California, the generally admired San Francisco vigilance committee of 1856, and the strong influence of California in Nevada, imitating a vigilance committee, or, at least, appropriating the name, was a likely development among the frontiersmen east of the Sierra.

Nevada, lacking any semblance of normal government institutions since the Mormon exodus, had both vigilantes and mobs. Washoe Valley, where Peleg had undergone such difficulties with claim jumpers, had developed an approximation of vigilantes. Each barn in the valley received a number. When action loomed, the "silent rider" made a circuit of the ranches in the valley saying only the number of the barn where the group would meet that night. They then rode to the tent of the offending squatter, piled the man with all his belongings and his family in his wagon, and slapped the reins across the horses' haunches. The stiffest resistance they encountered came from a squatter's wife who, according to an early settler, "screamed, struggled, spit, scratched, and swore" throughout the proceedings. Honey Lake Valley had no similar organization, but William ("Rough") Elliott gathered a mob there (which did not include the founding father Isaac Roop or the Honey Lake sheriff). On a June night in 1858 riders thundered toward the Carson Valley from the north.[12]

Their unlikely target was that popular and prominent local citizen Lucky Bill. In late March or early April a murder had taken place at Honey Lake. A French settler of means, Henri Gordier, had acquired a fine herd of Durham cattle from the departing Mormons, and Lucky Bill reportedly made a trip to Honey Lake to discuss purchasing them. An escaped murderer and former stage robber, Bill Edwards and an accomplice, John Mullen, went riding with Gordier, and Mullen shot him. They then burned the Frenchman's clothes in a nearby Indian dwelling and sank his body in a deep hole in the river. Ironically, of the men who would later be executed for this crime, Mullen, who had actually fired the deadly bullet and presently disappeared for parts unknown, would not be one of them. Although several Honey Lakers camping nearby heard the shot, nothing happened for a surprisingly long time. Edwards loaned and rented out the Gordier herd, probably availed himself of the valuables the Frenchman had brought from the

California gold country, and let it be known that Gordier had returned to France. Finally, early in May the lonely hearts of Honey Lake commandeered several passing emigrant Mormon women into a dance, where they started talking about Gordier's disappearance when they weren't clumping about the floor. They commenced a search, which ended after a good deal of difficulty when they pulled the ghastly remains of Gordier from the river.[13]

Edwards, sensing that he was under suspicion, fled to the Carson Valley to seek the protection of Lucky Bill, who hid him in the Sierra Nevada. "All men were human beings to Lucky Bill and he treated them all with equal kindness," according to his neighbor Thomas Knott. "He didn't inquire whether they were horse thieves or Mormon tithing collectors. His station was a rendezvous where the weary found rest, and the hungry never were turned from his door." This time, however, his predictable kindness to an underdog in flight who had sworn he was innocent would give his enemies an ax to use against him.[14]

Once started, events unrolled with surprising speed. Rough Elliott, the ringleader, convinced the Honey Lakers that Lucky Bill had engineered Gordier's murder in order to acquire his cattle herd. A mob began riding south to meet Elliott in the Carson Valley, picking up additional men in Washoe Valley. It is significant that these men were Honey Lakers, not residents of the Carson Valley, where Lucky Bill had many friends, and it is doubtful that a mob could have been raised against him. And significant as well that Lucky Bill's close and influential ally, Uncle Billy Rogers, was away in California. The involvement of the Masons and of Lucky Bill's local rivals, William Ormsby and "Old Dutch Fred" Dangberg, remains unclear. Before dawn the mob gathered around Lucky Bill's house and called him out. Seeing Elliott at the head of the crowd, Lucky Bill remarked, "My life is not worth a bit," and made no resistance. His wife, Maria, always dressed in white like a ghost, made a passionate plea for the couple's seventeen-year-old son, Jerome, arrested with his father. She spoke no word on behalf of her husband. Carson Valley people awoke to find Genoa full of armed men and surrounded so that no one could ride out to sound an alarm.[15]

D. R. Hawkins later said that the guards permitted his father and himself to visit Lucky Bill where they had hustled him, bound, in the hotel. When Hawkins's father, clearly surprised at seeing one of the valley's founding fathers in such a predicament, asked what this was all about, Lucky Bill answered: "These men have come here to hang me, and I guess they are going to do it." Gambler that he was, he knew "his luck was gonen that the cards was stocked on him," as one observer later put it. Fearing that Lucky Bill's Carson Valley friends might try to free him and possibly getting wind of the rumor (which proved false) that Rogers was riding from California with a hundred men, the Elliott mob moved their prisoner to the Sides Ranch at Clear Creek in Eagle Valley, a more defensible location. Also, they could count on the ill will of Sides and his comrades toward Lucky Bill. After the Sides gang successfully resisted the sheriff's sale of the ranch in 1856, they had tried and failed to drive Lucky Bill from his ranch and later threatened to banish Lucky Bill and his mistress, Martha Lamb. The Elliott crowd could be sure of a warm reception.[16]

The mob then made several other arrests. These included Lute Olds, one of three brothers, close friends of Lucky Bill, who reputedly had traveled west with him from Michigan and taken up residence at the base of Horsethief Canyon. The name was apt because the Olds brothers made their living by stealing emigrant stock, driving the animals up the canyon to fatten in the high meadows, and later herding them down again to sell to other emigrants, an occupation apparently regarded as legitimate in the valley. Olds and the others had no known connection to Gordier's murder, however, and the mob was more anxious to seize Bill Edwards. They tried to persuade Jerome Thorington to reveal Edwards's hiding place. Jerome resisted. But Lucky Bill told his son that Edwards could clear him, and the mob leaders promised to free Jerome and go easy on his father if he would betray Edwards.

[102]

Although the Honey Lakers denied it, some say they also promised to free Lucky Bill. Jerome reluctantly agreed and tricked Edwards into descending from his mountain hiding place.[17]

How false were these promises was quickly revealed. Jerome, having served his purpose, was freed, while Lucky Bill was tried and sentenced to death in a kangaroo court with the trappings of legal formality and none of the reality. Justice of the Peace Henry Van Sickle called it a "mock court." No evidence had suggested any connection with the crime beyond hiding Edwards. But the mob, according to the *Sacramento Bee*, had sworn in advance that Lucky Bill would never leave their hands alive, most of the jurors were drawn from their ranks, and they had no interest in evidence. While the jury met, hammering sounds rang out signifying the construction of the gallows. Lucky Bill and Maria parted without emotion, and he commended her to Jerome's care. When Martha Lamb, sobbing and calling a curse upon his captors, came to see him, he rattled his chains in his eagerness for a last embrace.[18]

As Lucky Bill waited in the wagon with the noose around his neck, some say he sang "The Last Rose of Summer," but that may have been only a bit of the folklore that had already started to gather around him. Others relate that he simply said, "I never lived like a hog and I ain't going to die like one." Young Lawrence Frey, through trickery, had drawn the short straw, making him driver of the wagon that would leave Lucky Bill dangling from the noose when the horses pulled away. The young man hesitated, tears running down his face, afraid to refuse yet unable to give the command that would end the life of his hero, Lucky Bill. Finally, Lucky Bill told him, "Drive out, boy," and it was over.[19]

The aftermath was brief. Jerome understandably had refused to shake the proffered hand of Rough Elliott. Lute Olds was fined and banished on pain of death, none of which anyone enforced with much rigor after the Honey Lakers returned to their usual haunts. The mob took Bill Edwards with them and hanged him there—perhaps. A story persists that he bought his life and fled to Mexico by revealing where he had cached the loot from an earlier stage robbery. Some even claimed to have heard from him in Mexico. This, too, may have been folklore, but the circumstance that after he was condemned he was taken back to Honey Lake instead of being hanged with Lucky Bill looks odd and suggests a plan to coerce information outside the field of vision of Carson Valley folk, especially in view of what they had done to Asa Snow shortly before riding down from Honey Lake. Snow was Mullen's hired man, and Edwards would swear that he was innocent of any responsibility. The Honey Lakers attempted to extort a confession from Snow by partially hanging him to show him how it felt. After his first dangle from the noose, Snow roundly cursed his captors. When he had been strung up a second time, Snow chewed them out again. The third time they waited too long, and Snow strangled before he could blister their ears with another outpouring of curses.[20]

The lynching of Lucky Bill continues to generate interest and confusion down to the present day. The Honey Lakers, from conviction or reluctance to admit a terrible error, clung to their belief in Lucky Bill's guilt; Carson Valleyites, for the most part, continued to believe him innocent, and their doubts seem plausible. After all, Lucky Bill was wealthy enough to have bought the Gordier herd if he had wanted it. Moreover, though he was a gambler and a sharp dealer, his past life showed that he was not a man who had used violence to gain his ends. The search for clarity is not aided by the report that Edwards changed his story and implicated Lucky Bill in the end, possibly in a last-ditch effort to gain clemency by telling the Honey Lakers what they wanted to hear. Because Lucky Bill had believed that Edwards's testimony would clear him, this version does not seem persuasive.[21]

In the murky realm of motives, one of the most cogent questions to pursue is "Who benefited?" Elliott appropriated Edwards's horse Bald

Hornet and the sizable amount of cash the fugitive carried. Still, although Bald Hornet was a racehorse well known in the Sierra Nevada, this does not seem sufficient cause to execute at least two men. Old Dutch Fred Dangberg, an 1857 arrival from Westphalia, took malicious pleasure almost fifty years later in regaining the Klauber Ranch, which he claimed Lucky Bill had wrested from him. Nonetheless, he was not the potent force in the valley that he would later become and played no important part in the lynching. Maria and Jerome inherited Lucky Bill's properties. Yet control of a considerable estate seems to have brought them little happiness. Jerome, disregarding his father's last admonitions, became a gambler, saloon keeper, and alcoholic and died in San Francisco at age thirty-seven. Maria finally went entirely mad and continued her perpetual lace making in a mental institution.[22]

Martha Lamb fared badly in the beginning and better in the end. Apart from the sale of her relative George Lamb's lands in 1859, she and the infant son she had christened William Thorington had no means of support. Yet this buxom, sturdy young beauty was no quitter. She got along somehow and several years later married David Olds, after his wife in Sacramento divorced him on grounds of committing adultery with Martha Lamb. Their descendants believe that "pressure from the community" drove the couple's departure from the Carson Valley. As David had no property either, he set off with Martha to make a new life in a new place. After trying the Walker River country, they decided on Round Valley, a little north of Bishop, California. The presence of many Indians in that area had deterred early settlement. There, in green meadows, in the shadow of the steepest, craggiest peaks of the Sierra Nevada, they developed a fine ranch and raised several children. Neither Martha's notoriety nor David's past in Horsethief Canyon prevented them from becoming popular and respected members of the community. Martha's warm hospitality drew people from miles around when a dance was held at the Olds ranch. Lucky Bill would have been amused could he have known that his grandson,

Cecil Thorington, became a sheriff—a reversal that would have meant laughter and several rounds of drinks for the boys at his old bar in Genoa.[23]

Although no one outside his family benefited financially from Lucky Bill's death, benefit could assume other forms. In the pages of the *Mountain Democrat*, John ("Jerry") Long, an Ormsby associate, admitted that Lucky Bill and Ormsby were enemies and attempted to quell the "prejudice and excitement" against Ormsby by insisting that Ormsby's only role in the lynching had been "searching out crime and bringing the guilty to trial," which indicated a larger part than Jerry probably realized. Long also claimed that a casual remark by Lucky Bill constituted a threat to assassinate Ormsby. This open acknowledgment of prejudice and excitement suggests that despite Ormsby's position in the background throughout the lynching, many in the Carson Valley suspected that he had been the mastermind behind the scenes. He did gain from Lucky Bill's death. Although the allegation that Lucky Bill headed a criminal gang can be dismissed as self-serving propaganda from the lynchers, he had been a focus of leadership in the loose faction of old settlers that Ormsby probably saw as an obstacle in his rise to power.[24]

All the same, at the end of the day, the question of motive centers on the driving force behind the lynching, Rough Elliott. Because the fragmentary history of the times records no quarrel between Elliott and Lucky Bill, the possibilities are necessarily conjectural. One is the primal emotion of envy. Lucky Bill was quite simply the tallest tree in the forest. From the viewpoint of Ormsby and Elliott, he was too successful, too popular, too contented, and, as the German philosopher Helmut Schoeck has argued, envy seeks not to acquire the possessions of the envied person but to destroy him. Perhaps in Elliott a hidden personal grudge lent force to envy. There is a ghost of a possibility that it may have started with gambling. So heavy a plunger was Elliott that three years later, the Washoe Valley mill in which he held an interest was nearly swamped by a flood of his gambling debts. Might he have

[106]

formerly gambled and lost to the professional who never lost—Lucky
Bill—and nursed a dream of revenge that blossomed when opportunity arose?[25]

If nothing else, the lynching of Lucky Bill had demonstrated the need
for strong governmental authority on the Nevada frontier. Although no
more bodies swung from the gallows left standing as a grisly warning,
the need became ever more apparent because the lynching and the
emergence of vigilantism sharpened the differences among Carson Valley settlers. Two opposed groups faced off, the vigilantes led by Ormsby
and the antivigilantes, also called the Mormons, a catchall term for old
settlers who opposed "government by the prejudice or caprices of an
irresponsible Junto." Within the year vigilance committee members
committed at least two unpunished homicides. The vigilantes apparently played with the idea of appropriating government functions by
electing their own officials and passing laws. The antivigilantes countered with a petition to territorial governor Cumming asking him to re-
organize Carson County. They aimed not to endorse control by Utah
but to replace rule by the vigilante junta with stronger federal authority
until Congress granted a separate territory.[26]

Governor Cumming responded in September by appointing a
Genoa merchant, John S. Child, probate judge for the eastern slope.
After Child called an election for October 30, the vigilantes immediately took steps to invalidate it in protest against Utah rule. They apparently believed that a demonstration of hopeless anarchy would
strengthen the thrust for territorial status. The vote totals recorded in
the election were minuscule: the most popular candidates received 58
votes, and several won by only 2–4 votes. The votes in five of seven
precincts, 104 ballots in all, were discarded for illegalities but would
hardly have increased the totals by much. While this exercise may
have strengthened the argument for a territory on grounds of anarchy,
it may also have raised doubts concerning the size of the population.[27]

Not so many years had passed since a much larger population was the standard for a territory.

Vigilante activity intensified. The elected sheriff, L. B. Abernathy, and the elected selectman, Richard Sides, both vigilantes and enemies of Lucky Bill who had played a prominent part in the lynching, then declined to serve in an effort to further undermine Utah law. On December 12 the vigilantes met, enacted resolutions denouncing Utah law, and designated a committee including Ormsby to inform Judge Child that they refused to acknowledge his authority. Facing what Child called "an open rebellion against the laws," the antivigilantes sent the records of Carson County to Governor Cumming by a trusted courier for safekeeping. Deputy Recorder Stephen A. Kinsey explained the rea-

Genoa, East Foot of Sierra Nevada, J. J. Young, 1859, depicting Captain J. H. Simpson's surveying party arriving in 1859. Courtesy of the Nevada State Museum, Carson City; and the National Archives, College Park, Md. (Cartographic Record, RG-77, CWMF, MISC. 120-7).

sons for this unusual action: "My object in sending the Records from this place is this, as I do not consider them safe here. Parties who are opposed to the Laws of Utah have held a meeting and appointed a committee of ten persons to obtain these Records by force and at all hazards." Not entirely intimidated, Child called a mass public meeting in Genoa on Christmas Eve to demonstrate how much support he could muster. But he prudently postponed convening court. Writing to Congressman Smith, Crane endeavored to turn this political bacchanal into an argument for creating a new territory by playing the Mormon card: "The only remedy for this unnatural war, now raging between the Mormons and the Anti-Mormons in Utah, is to be found in the immediate separation of these people under two distinct governmental organizations. One thing is inevitable—the Mormons and Anti-Mormons will never, and can never live together in peace, under one government."[28]

⚜

At the close of 1858, Nevada had tumbled downhill into a worse condition than when the year began. Economically, the exodus of the industrious Mormons to Utah and the less industrious prospectors to the Fraser River excitement had hurt, and one traveler at Genoa described it as "decaying." Isolation had decreased when a telegraph line from Placerville reached Genoa, though another three years would pass before it extended to Salt Lake City. In addition to this leap forward in communications, the Lewis Brady Company bought the old Pioneer line, and in season twice-weekly stages from Placerville to Genoa began bumping and rumbling up the rough road over the Sierra Nevada to connect with the Overland stage from Salt Lake City bearing the eastern mail. Undaunted by his harrowing experiences on the Great Basin route, George Chorpenning had won the mail contract. When winter snows closed the mountain passes, Chorpenning's associate Snowshoe Thompson brought the mail through on a regular basis with sleighs and ski couriers. The final sign of changes that would tie Nevadans more closely to the world and to each other came in December. Publication began of Nevada's first real newspaper, the *Territorial Enterprise,* printed on an actual though venerable press, unlike its handwritten predecessors.[29]

Yet the news that now traveled more swiftly across the Sierra Nevada was hardly good. Politically, Nevada had spiraled downward into vigilantism and lynch law. Though clearly the sensible course for the nation, the rapprochement between Brigham Young and the U.S. government had weakened the drive for territorial status. More than one observer, however, noted signals that some, at least, believed the new territory to be imminent. Newspaper correspondent Tennessee wrote in his dispatch:

> We have had, during the past few months, several distinguished arrivals in these parts, of well dressed gentlemen from California, whose object it is (so they say) to build for themselves homes in this beautiful country. Being unable to discover any sign of house or habitation built by their industrious hands . . . the knowing ones have at length found out that they are nothing less than unfortunate office seekers. . . . I believe they are laboring under the impression that the coming session of Congress will be held for no other purpose than to establish the Territory of Nevada, so as to create offices for them to fill.[30]

8

Bonanza, 1859

HE WINTER OF 1858–1859 was the worst that anyone remembered. It began with a hard and lasting freeze that deprived the Gold Canyon miners of the water they needed to run their Long Toms. Then it snowed and snowed and snowed. Tennessee opined that snow had piled so high in the Carson Valley that "we would have to . . . borrow a deep sea line, in order to ascertain its profundity." Peleg Brown wrote his parents at the end of March that it was still blowing and snowing "as usual." The trails across the Sierra Nevada closed, even disappeared in some stretches. One of the few advantages of the heavy snows was the recovery of Peleg's stolen horses. With his neighbor, he followed the horses' trail to the Sierra Nevada and found the animals abandoned there because the thieves had been unable to take them across the snowbound mountains.[1]

No wagons or pack trains could cross either, and the *Territorial Enterprise* suspended publication for lack of paper. Storms downed the telegraph. Even Snowshoe Thompson was fazed, and the mail was long delayed. Shortages grew more acute; prices rose, with flour reaching fifty dollars a barrel when any could be found. These privations became intolerable when whiskey, "that great staple" at the settlements, ran out. A determined effort by the citizenry to open a trail resulted. Still, the first pack train was unable to struggle over the mountain passes until early May.[2]

[111]

The Indians, crouched over low fires of sagebrush coals in flimsy reed huts with the icy wind whistling through the cracks, suffered most terribly. The piñon harvest on which they depended had been unusually poor. Game was scarce, hunted and driven away by the influx of newcomers with herds of stock. Many Indians starved or froze to death. Inevitably, they killed a few of the Truckee Meadows ranchers' two thousand head of stock for food. Also inevitably, they died from eating the meat poisoned with strychnine that the ranchers put out for wolf bait. And inevitably, the ill feeling between Indians and settlers increased. The Indians ascribed their misery to the witchcraft of malevolent beings, the settlers. Although Tennessee urged "a proper spirit of charity" toward "these poor outdoor wanderers," charity was in short supply, even from Peleg who had formerly gotten along rather well with the Indians. He wrote his sister Lydia that if Indian stock thefts did not cease, "wee shell raise a company and clean them out root and branch."[3]

That spring no sign had yet appeared of the momentous event at hand. Tennessee found the times "very dull" (except, of course, for the occasional homicide). Elzy Knott, a handsome and popular young man in the Carson Valley, had been shot and killed in a trivial dispute over a bridle. His grief-stricken father, millwright Thomas Knott, blamed the tragedy on the Mormons, as he did all misfortunes other than the weather. Miner William Sides knifed another miner, John "Pike" Jessup. Peleg Brown, who served as a "jeuror," wrote, "It was proved to bea willfull murder there being to jeurors bribed in consequence he was bailed. . . . He has already left the valley I think it doubtfull if he come back any more." Tennessee courageously observed that vigilantes or those connected with them who committed crimes always went unpunished. The winter ruckus between the Gold Canyon miners and the Chinese placering at present Dayton (then known as Chinatown) had apparently subsided. As the massive snows melted, the Carson River flooded, covering an estimated quarter of the valley. Yet the traders and ranchers had some cause for optimism after this winter that would not die. They anticipated that bountiful grass along the trails would mean plenty of emigrants and a boost to their languishing trade. Nonetheless, the emigrant trade would soon cease to be the staff of life on the eastern slope because the Gold Canyon miners were finally blundering onto the Comstock Lode. Necessity, rather than a keener grasp of geology, finally pushed them toward higher ground. Gold Canyon was played out. They could glean no more from the leavings of the spiderweb of small gold veins that netted the hills around present Silver City and fed the canyon, and their earnings had sunk to two dollars a day.[4]

When out hunting, James "Old Virginny" Finney noticed a little yellow hill at the head of Gold Canyon and apparently thought yellow equaled gold. He was considered a good prospector when sober. On January 28, 1859, he returned to the spot with a few friends. They scraped away the snow, panned a little of the yellowish dirt, and thought it promising enough to record placer claims. Lemuel "Sandy" Bowers, Henry Comstock, and others located an adjoining claim, but most of the Gold Canyon crowd thought Finney's little yellow hill a poor prospect. After the snows retreated in spring, Finney and the others began washing the dirt in their rockers and crushing chunks of decomposed quartz with surprisingly good results. About ten feet down they broke into a vein of red-tinged quartz laced with gold (later known as the Old Red Ledge). Fixated upon gold, they named the site Gold Hill, and two or three years would pass before the rich mines developed there, including the Belcher, Crown Point, and Yellow Jacket, were recognized as silver mines. Although they did not know it, these prospectors had struck the southern end of the Comstock Lode, and there is a certain symmetry in the circumstance that Finney, the first known permanent settler on the eastern slope, was the one to do it.[5]

Despite their initial skepticism, the Gold Canyon crowd based at Johntown presently decamped to Gold Hill. Two Irish miners, Peter O'Riley and Pat McLaughlin, worked at the top of the ravine where the mountain slope begins to rise. So poor were the returns that they

Miners working at Gold Hill, 1859. From Dan De Quille, *The Big Bonanza*, p. 22.

planned to depart for the Walker River diggings after they accumulated a few more days' earnings. Then, about four feet down on June 1, the trench they had been opening struck a mass of black decomposed material spangled with gold. Although their earnings soon skyrocketed to one hundred dollars or more per day, they distrusted this strange off-color metal, more the shade of silver than the familiar placer gold.[6]

Henry P. Comstock, who rode by on a mustang pony the first evening of their discovery, instantly set about to get a piece of it. Even in a crowd where eccentricity was not unusual, the tall, lanky Comstock stood out as an odd duck. The miners called him "Old Pancake," though he was only thirty-nine, because he always declared himself too busy to bake bread and instead fried pancakes. Indeed, he was busy, speculating, dreaming, and buying into everything, whether he had the money to pay or not. By his own account, he had been hunting and trapping in the wilderness since childhood and had fought in the Black Hawk and Mexican American Wars. He came into the Carson Valley in 1856 driving a herd of sheep, most of which the Indians stole. He went on to Gold Canyon and mined at American Flat—at least, the Indians he employed worked there.[7]

Dismounting from his mustang and examining the McLaughlin-O'Riley discovery, Comstock at once insisted that he had claimed the area as ranch land and therefore deserved a share of their claim. And what was more, he held the water right to the spring on which they depended, so he and his partner, Immanuel ("Manny") Penrod, should have a hundred-foot section (the future Mexican Mine) set aside for themselves. Comstock's claim to ownership through ranch land was decidedly shaky, but the Irishmen acceded to his demands. Had they been less generous and openhanded, had they realized the fabulous value of their discovery, had they not been a little afraid of trouble with Comstock because he was considered half mad, they might have offered more resistance. As author Charles Shinn has observed, Comstock "never really found anything, but he claimed everything in sight." Ironically, the great Comstock Lode was named for "one of the most ignorant and bombastic of men."[8]

In this way, the lode was discovered on both its northern and its southern ends by placer miners who did not realize that its riches lay in silver. Manny Penrod related that when O'Riley and McLaughlin set up a primitive arrastra (a circular stone bowl in which a weight dragged by a circling mule crushed ore), the Mexican who ran it would say, "No good per arrastra, mucha plata." McLaughlin would answer, "Damn your plata! We want the gold in it." Only the unnamed Mexican recognized rich sulfides of silver where the others saw only troublesome black stuff, which they threw away as worthless waste. William Dolman later voiced a thought that must have been commonly felt among the old Gold Canyon crowd when the Comstock was well on its way to producing nearly $350 million worth of ore over the years, "I had tramped over one of the richest treasures of the earth, but a few yards under my feet, and knew it not."[9]

During that fateful June, the discoverers may not have understood what they had, but they knew they had something, and a tingle of excitement began to shiver through the eastern slope. Miners abandoned their prospects and ranchers deserted their stock as they hastened to the scene to stake claims. On June 27 a ranch hand doing a favor for a Truckee Meadows station keeper brought a sample of the blackish rock to be assayed in Grass Valley, California. When the first assay seemed unbelievable, he gave the sample to Judge James Walsh, a miner and mill owner, and Walsh tried a different assayer. The results were even more astonishing—at $3,876 a ton, three-quarters silver and one-quarter gold. Still incredulous, Walsh turned to a noted Irish expert for advice. The advice he received was unequivocal: head over the mountains as soon as possible. On horseback with his partner, Joseph Woodworth, Walsh rode out early the next morning, by no means too soon.[10]

As Comstock journalist Dan De Quille related only half humorously:

> It was agreed among the few who knew the result of the assay that the matter should, for the time being, be kept a profound secret. . . . But each man had intimate friends in whom he had the utmost confidence . . . and these bosom friends soon knew that a silver-mine of wonderful richness had been discovered over in the Washoe country. These again had their friends, and, although the result of the assay . . . was not ascertained until late at night, by nine o'clock the next morning half the town of Grass Valley knew the wonderful news.[11]

The rush to Washoe, as they then called it, had started, and the eastern slope would never be the same.

The radical change in Peleg Brown's fortunes that followed shows the scope of the transformation. Already on June 18 he noted "great excitement" over the rich gold deposits at the "new mines" only twelve miles from his ranch and people coming through every day. Within the month, as the rush from California gained force, he began "ceeping a kind of hotell now there is so much excitement about the diggins causing so much travle this being the last plaice whare they can get water and grass before they reach the mines." He sold them milk and butter and also provided meals. Peleg's ranch, soon a stage station, had the ideal location for boomers arriving from California over Donner Pass and heading for Virginia City via Dutch Flat and Crystal Peak. As traffic increased, the primitive horse path climbing the Virginia Range would become the improved but still precipitous Brown toll road (now Geiger Grade).[12]

In addition to the men he needed to hire to run his thriving enterprise, Peleg gained more help and much comfort with the long-awaited arrival of his brother Joshua with his wife and daughters and a herd of stock considerably diminished by losses while crossing the Plains ("I think Joshua wont try the plains any more"). When he rode east on the trail to meet the family at the Humboldt, Peleg found that Joshua had been gone from camp for several days in an effort to recover thirty-three head of cattle stolen by Indians ("You cant half imagine how glad Jane was to sea me as well as I did them"). Joshua succeeded in retrieving the stock, and soon the family was safely ensconced in Peleg's "very venteleted house." No more would Peleg be "loathsome at times."[13]

By fall Peleg was bubbling with great expectations. Testing had demonstrated the worth of the new mines, so "there cant bea no humbug abot them," he assured his younger brother Pardon. Soon, "money will bea as plenty as in Calfornia [in] the year of 49." Happily, he wrote about the high prices prevailing: "11 cents orn foot" for beef, 10 cents a pound for potatoes, 16 dollars for a hundredweight of flour. He planned a large and lucrative garden with potatoes and melons and a planting of fruit trees in the spring; he needed to do a good deal of fencing to separate his increasingly valuable stock from other herds grazing in the meadows; he hoped to squeeze in a trip to southern

California to drive up a bunch of Spanish horses; he expected to make $3,000 or $4,000 from his hotel in the coming year (more than $80,000 in today's dollars). His original intention to sell out in four or five years after making his fortune and return to Rhode Island because "I have but one life to live" had not yet been wholly abandoned, and he continued to write from time to time of visiting his family. But he kept postponing the date. For a young man who found himself in "the finest plaice in the valley" in the midst of a mining rush, there was simply too much to do.[14]

Not all on the eastern slope viewed the quickening rush as happily as Peleg—at least not yet, not with winter coming on and snow likely to close the passes and leave everyone on even shorter rations than during the previous winter. The weather soon worsened ominously, with a spell of severe cold that turned the Carson Valley into a "great boneyard" where "numbers of cattle and horses are frozen to death every night." Promising though it was, the Comstock remained in the early stages of development. The Maldonado brothers, Gabriel, Francisco, and Epistacio, relied on little adobe furnaces to smelt ores from the Mexican Mine, and primitive arrastras continued in use. Autumn arrived before a $112,000 shipment of ore from the Ophir was brought by mules and wagons over the Sierra Nevada, by train from Folsom to Sacramento, and by riverboat to San Francisco, where its display aroused a hubbub among the Californians, ever susceptible to new mining excitements. This was exactly what the old residents would have liked to avoid. Abandoning the usual role of mining camp journalists, namely, the unstinting praise of any new discovery however minuscule, newspapermen strove to dampen the enthusiasm. The *Territorial Enterprise* warned of "unhealthy excitement," and Tennessee wrote of the privations awaiting newcomers.[15]

Although no definitive figure on the population at the close of 1859 exists and many of the early boomers had left in disappointment, the numbers on the eastern slope had certainly grown, and perhaps even doubled. No disagreement exists on the conditions that this increase

A 1907 photo of Peleg Brown's Greek Revival–style ranch house at the "finest plaice in the valley," constructed in 1864 to replace his earlier "very venteleted" dwelling. Fourteen small bedrooms on the second floor accommodated travelers to the Comstock and boarders. Owned by Benjamin Damonte, the house is now on the register of National Historic Places. Courtesy Benjamin Damonte.

produced. Tennessee reported: "Genoa is so full of people that no less than thirty or forty individuals—unable to procure lodgings elsewhere—nightly resort to the hayloft over the livery stable." The luckier ones crowded twelve to a room in small houses. Food prices skyrocketed again, and rather than pay top dollar for feed, many found it cheaper to let their stock freeze to death (unlike Peleg, who watched over every animal). Three towns had sprung up on the Comstock, Gold Hill, Silver City, and Virginia City, appropriately named for "Old

Virginny" Finney after interest in naming the town for Chief Winnemucca subsided.[16]

But the word *towns* suggests a level of dignity at odds with the
primitive reality. The boomers sheltered themselves in tents, mud and
stone hovels, mine tunnels, and holes in the ground. Those in lodging
houses fared little better, sleeping on shelflike bunks extending from
floor to ceiling, chairs, tables, counters, and floors and paying a dollar
a night for the privilege. The Comstocker Henry DeGroot recalled:
"Frequently the gales that came tearing down the sides of Mount
Davidson would, in the middle of the night, when all were wrapt in
sweet slumber . . . rend to tatters their canvass dormitory . . . leaving
the hapless sleepers exposed to the peltings of the pitiless storm . . .
howling and swearing as they sought to screen their half-naked persons under the fluttering fragments of their disruptured tabernacle."[17]

Yet they persisted—having no choice, because a return to California
over he snowbound Sierra Nevada was no longer an option—and their
presence signified an important shift in the population. From the time
that John Reese rolled his wagons into the Carson Valley in 1851, the
settlers on the eastern slope had been primarily traders and ranchers.
Now the center of gravity had shifted to the miners, no longer a lesser
component but the central force that would shape the character of the
region and the state still aborning. For the Indians, suffering through
another cruel winter, it mattered little if the influx of white men were
traders or miners. Their growing numbers raised a stark question:
could two peoples survive in this harsh land?

The usual mind-set of the prospector is to get rich and get out. Ac-
cordingly, to most of the men camped in the hills, questions of governmental jurisdiction held little interest, provided that no one interfered
with mining. In fact, they were hoping and subsisting on the western
edge of Utah Territory, and in January Utah had made ineffectual ges-
tures to assert control by reorganizing Carson County, allowing it a
representative in the territorial legislature, and compounding it with
two other counties in a U.S. judicial district. Crane's optimistic predic-

tions and diligent lobbying had come to naught, and the territorial bill had not passed. In a March 2 letter, he explained the reasons to his constituents "with very considerable pain": Congress had been distracted by the slavery issue and other matters, the president lacked political influence in Congress, the Speaker of the House had been unfavorably disposed, and none of the territorial bills had passed. Undaunted, he had "no doubt" of success in the next session. "Let us not despair." he urged the Nevadans. "Pick up the flint and fire again."[18]

Crane took his own advice and fired again with an announcement of his candidacy for reelection. Tennessee waspishly noted that Crane's arrival "was received with some enthusiasm by two or three friends" and he had departed for Carson City "where he also has an admirer." According to Tennessee, who favored another candidate, his campaign rally in Carson City failed to draw an audience. Nonetheless, he campaigned hard, speaking in Genoa and Gold Hill and making the rather difficult journey to the Walker River diggings. The voting took place in July with disputed results.[19]

More important political developments were afoot than the election of an unofficial delegate to Congress. Local delegates had also been chosen for a convention, supposedly "to consider the public safety"; the actual purpose was to spur Congress into action by writing a constitution and organizing a provisional government, a device resorted to by settlers in at least eight other localities. Understandably, since many of those present were old Californians, the document they produced resembled California's constitution. The principal innovation appeared in a declaration of the causes for separation from Utah. The idea of establishing a government before becoming a territory did not meet with universal approbation. Tennessee saw the provisional government as a front for the vigilante mob that only "scheming demagogues or an ignorant rabble" would approve. The Walker River delegation rejected its authority. Yet the almost universal detestation of Mormon control worked in favor of an alternate government. In the words of the *Territorial Enterprise*, the settlers sought freedom from

"all connection with an ignorant, besotted, and priest-ridden community, with whom we have not one feeling in common—from the tyran-
nical enactments of the Utah Legislature—under which we will never
live—from the bigoted, mind-enslaving despotism of Mormon theocracy." The voters approved the constitution in September; Crane had
already secured a tenuous hold on his office when the convention under the influence of William Ormsby and his friends canvassed the
vote and gave the victory to Crane amid allegations of fraud on both
sides. According to Tennessee, Crane's principal rival, Indian agent
Major Frederick Dodge, had received a majority of 150 in the popular
vote. As historian Russell Elliott has pointed out, Nevada now had
three governments—provisional, Utah Territorial, and federal—and
the result was chaos.[20]

In late August the federal element arrived in the person of U.S. District Judge John Cradlebaugh, possibly the closest thing to a hero to
appear on the eastern slope. Ohio born, six feet tall, and a widower at
forty, Cradlebaugh was much admired for his fearless efforts when
serving in Utah to investigate Mormon responsibility for the Mountain Meadows Massacre. These efforts had been frustrated by the
Mormons at every turn, leaving the judge with scant regard for Mormons. Upon his arrival in Genoa, the town received him with firing
cannons and "every demonstration of joy." In early October Cradlebaugh convened court in Genoa in a second-floor room that could be
accessed only by ladder, but legal talents new to the region made the
climb. Long-standing quarrels were resolved, and settlers who sued to
recoup fines they had been forced to pay to the vigilance committee received satisfaction in Cradlebaugh's court. Tennessee anticipated trouble from "the prevailing faction" because Cradlebaugh favored neither
the vigilantes nor the provisional government, and some saw him as
an arm of Utah control, despite his position as a federal official.[21]

Cradlebaugh's agenda, which Tennessee proclaimed the noblest
purpose that ever actuated any man, was sweeping. He envisaged the
political extermination of the Mormons by means that reversed Orson

Hyde's plan to "secure, secure" the eastern slope by swamping Gentile voters with Mormons. Watching the rapid population increase taking place before his eyes, Cradlebaugh believed that the Gentiles of the eastern slope would soon be able to outvote all the Mormons in Utah, win the legislature, and move the capital. If this could be accomplished, it would be far more detrimental to church rule than merely separating the western portion of Utah Territory because the loss of the entire territory to the Gentiles would mean that the Mormons would have no territory at all. In December, after court adjourned, Cradlebaugh departed for Washington to promote his plan by urging the repeal of the organic act creating Utah Territory. In the midst of a mining rush, with memories of California's transformation still green, many things suddenly seemed possible.[22]

Meanwhile, newspaper reportage on the fraudulent election and the looming possibility that Major Dodge was likely to present his rival credentials in Washington may have taken a toll on James Crane. Possibly he drank to excess. The Dodge faction called him "a mere whiskey bloat, spending his time at the bars which are the most popular institution in the territory." On a late September evening in Gold Hill, Crane was seated at a table conversing with a friend when he suddenly threw up his hands and exclaimed, "A great change has come over me." The change was death. He keeled over dead at the age of forty, whether from a massive heart attack or a stroke is not clear. Although he had failed to carry the day, an assessment of his career concluded that his assiduous lobbying in Washington had "prepared the way" for territorial status.[23] He was an old pioneer, a bore, a visionary, and Nevada's first representative to Congress.

Because Ormsby and his friends declined to accept Major Dodge, another election was held on November 12 in which the office went to Colonel John J. Musser, a California lawyer given to spouting oratory flowery enough to have embarrassed even the late Crane. Then an unexpected roadblock developed. Alfred James, clerk of the federal district court and former editor of the *Territorial Enterprise*, refused to canvass the November 12 election because he maintained that Dodge was Nevada's legally elected representative (a stance in which Judge Cradlebaugh may have had a hand). The response was a Carson City meeting chaired by Ormsby on November 21 at which those present appointed their own clerk, who obediently certified Musser. They then proceeded to compose yet another memorial to Congress.[24]

In several ways, however, the last meeting of the year on December 10 held more significance. Although it had been known for years that Honey Lake was in California, the proponents of the provisional government, with typical disregard for boundaries and rules, had made Isaac Roop, the founding father of Honey Lake, their governor. Because few members of the legislature had assembled, Roop adjourned the body until the following July and declared in a December 15 proclamation that "an organization of the Provisional Government, would, at the present time, be impolitic." The provisional government, believed to be a front for the vigilantes, had effectively collapsed.[25]

Still more significantly, Ormsby, who had presided over previous meetings, was absent, and a new name appeared in the position of chair, W. Stewart. This was William Morris Stewart, the brilliant, charismatic California lawyer and leader of men whom Mark Twain described as "a long-legged, bull-headed, whopper jawed . . . monomaniac." Stewart would play a substantial part in writing the Nevada constitution, mastermind the U.S mining law that stands to this day, serve the California railroad bosses disgracefully, and reign as Nevada's perpetual U.S. senator for most of the latter nineteenth century. Ormsby's stature was rapidly shrinking by comparison.[26]

Indeed, as the mining rush gained momentum, Ormsby's position left much to be desired. He had done well in real estate. On Crane's suggestion, he had led in the development of Carson City as the future Nevada state capital. He owned a hotel there, a store in Johntown, and various other interests. He was able to clothe his wife in rose-colored French jacquard silk and lace. But he had missed out on the Comstock, despite many opportunities. He had failed to carry through when William Dolman and others who were the first to work quartz in the region asked him to obtain an assay for them. He had not bought in when the early prospectors began selling their claims cheaply and speed was of the essence. James Walsh, the Grass Valley miner and mill owner, had moved quickly to gain control of the Ophir Mine, half the California, and other interests when the first assays came in. George Hearst, with lightning speed, optioned McLaughlin's interest, the basis of his future fortune. Gabriel Maldonado bought half the Mexican Mine from Manny Penrod. The Winters boys, ranchers from Washoe Valley, bought a piece of the new mines. In August California miner John Mackay and his partner packed their blankets and walked one hundred miles to the latest excitement. Both were dead broke, but in time Mackay would become the prime organizer of the fabled Bonanza Firm and the acknowledged king of the Comstock. To regain his former eminence, William Ormsby would need to do something spectacular.[27]

9

An Indian for Breakfast and a Pony to Ride, 1860

THEY WAITED, with mounting impatience. On the Comstock they waited, sporadically attempting to scrape away several feet of snow and resume prospecting. In Placerville they waited for the Sierra Nevada snows to retreat. The peripatetic journalist J. Ross Browne, on his way to the place they called Washoe, vividly described the Placerville scene in March: "Every hotel and restaurant was full to overflowing. The streets were blocked up with crowds of adventurers all bound for Washoe. The gambling and drinking saloons were crammed to suffocation with customers practicing for Washoe. . . . Mexican *vaqueros* were driving headstrong mules through the streets on the road to Washoe. . . . In short, there was nothing but Washoe to be seen, heard, or thought of." Some who could not wait had earlier braved the crossing by laying blankets on the snow for their mules to step on. Fortunately for the eager horde, they faced only ten feet of snow in the Sierra Nevada, with drifts thirty to sixty feet deep, and a blanket of snow on the valleys for only one hundred days.[1]

Unable to hire a horse, Browne decided to backpack and set out on foot regardless of the lingering snowstorms. At each inn along the way, he rushed with a stampeding crowd to get a meal when a sitting was called. Finding the accommodations worse than the weather as he neared the summit, he continued through the falling snow, repeatedly stumbling into deep holes made by floundering mules. "It was a constant struggle through melted snow and mud," he wrote, "slipping, sliding, grasping, rolling, tumbling." Undeterred and finding no accommodations in Hope Valley, he continued to forge forward through heavy wind and blinding sleet before emerging in the Carson Valley, which he disparaged as "barren in the extreme." This assessment contradicted the summer emigrants arriving from the Forty Mile Desert who thought it a paradise and may have reflected the contrast with the wildflower-strewn meadows of the western Sierra Nevada foothills through which he had passed. It also tallied with Tennessee's criticism of recent neglectful ranching practices. When Browne later observed hundreds of carcasses of starved cattle littering the valley, with thousands of gorged buzzards in attendance, the hellish spectacle did not improve his opinion of the place.[2]

As Browne continued on his journey, he gave Carson City a nod ("quite a pretty and thrifty little town"), but when he arrived at the "far-famed Virginia City," he found it "essentially infernal in every aspect." Its haphazard scattering of tents, shanties, and coyote holes amid the mud appalled him not less than its climate of "hurricanes and snow" and its unwashed polyglot population. Although he had little to say about the mines, not yet operating at full throttle until the winter snows subsided, he noticed knots of avid speculators "huddled around the corners, in earnest consultation about the rise and fall of stocks."[3]

When Browne once more traversed the Sierra Nevada, racing to find a wide place in the narrow trail to avoid being tumbled into the canyon each time another pack train of mules attended by lustily cursing vaqueros came pounding along, he found San Franciscans in an even greater fever of anxiety over mining stocks. Because the San Francisco stock exchange that was to "make the market" on Nevada mining stocks for half a century had not yet been organized, all the action took place on the street. Browne could not take a step without being buttonholed by a panicky investor wanting to know if the Comstock was another humbug.[4]

Investors anxious for news of the mines besiege journalist J. Ross Browne upon his return to San Francisco from the Comstock. From J. Ross Browne, *A Peep at Washoe and Washoe Revisited*, p. 125.

The fact was that less than a year after its discovery and only a season after that discovery became known in California, the Comstock was experiencing its first stock bust. Values plummeted. Investors scurried about the streets in a vain effort to unload their stocks but could find no buyers. Although time would show the fabulous values on the Comstock, these lay in only a handful of mines, and many claims of the sixteen thousand ultimately filed in the region had been sold for fancy prices without ever being developed. The panic had followed newspaper reports that base metals had been found. As the *Territorial Enterprise* delicately phrased it, doubts had been sown by parties "for sinister purposes." Browne, less delicately, openly declared that these parties had been "bucking down" the stock for speculative reasons. Both factors probably figured in Tennessee's somber conclusion that "there will be more money lost than made" in the months ahead.[5]

Worse was still to come. Until 1860 the Great Basin had seemed an island of relative peace in the Indian wars. No army units were stationed on the eastern slope. The map showing Nevada as the largest swath of unceded Indian territory in the United States obliquely reflected the circumstance that the U.S. government probably had not considered the Washo, the Paiutes, and the Shoshone numerous and dangerous enough to necessitate treaty negotiations, nor had they acknowledged that this large territory belonged to the Indians. Wars raged to the south in New Mexico Territory, where two hundred to three hundred settlers had been killed, nearly a million dollars' worth of livestock lost, and close to a thousand Navaho attacked Fort Defiance; genocide raged in northern California, where mobs had exterminated entire tribes; more battles raged in the Northwest, where the army fought the Rogue River Indians and the Yakamas and also sometimes protected the Indians from volunteers bent on extermination; farther east, in Idaho Territory, an attack by Bannocks and Shoshone upon the Mormons at Lemhi forced abandonment of the settlement. When all was said and done, 90 percent of the killings by Indians of nearly four hundred emigrants on the western trails fell west of South Pass in Wyoming Territory, deaths in which the aggressive Bannocks had played a part. Though some emigrants died in the Nevada deserts, stock raids were the norm there, and it appears that Indian casualties substantially exceeded whites.[6]

Several elements had combined to create this relatively tranquil situation. Unlike Plains tribes such as the Sioux among whom distinction in warfare was an honor proudly sought, war played little part among the Nevada tribes. Survival in a harsh desert environment occupied most Paiute energies, and they had no warrior fraternities comparable to the Cheyenne dog soldiers. Their legends included a battle against red-haired cannibals, more recently they had fought the California Pitt River Indians, and occasionally they raided the Shoshone for horses and women, but war did not loom large in their culture. As Sarah Winnemucca put it, the Paiutes "are not fond of going to war." This ethos was strengthened by the peace policies of two influential Paiute leaders, old Chief Truckee and his son-in-law, Winnemucca. At least twice Truckee had turned his people away from retaliatory attacks. Winnemucca calmed tensions on several occasions, and both leaders favored adaptation to the white world that had surged over them. Although the Paiutes were never as formally organized in ranked positions of authority as whites imagined, Winnemucca enjoyed wide respect from both whites and Indians. Moreover, these leaders understood the nature of the opposition. Truckee, a noted emigrant guide, had fought with John Charles Frémont in the Bear Flag revolt, and both had taken some of their people with them to spend time in California. Unlike more isolated tribes farther east such as the Bannock, they grasped the fundamental truth in all the Indian wars of the West that would ultimately defeat the Indians, no matter how brave, no matter how skilled in battle: Indians could not begin to match the numbers and resources of the white man.[7]

In 1860 these restraints on both sides began to snap. Whites had been restrained by their inferior numbers, probably half those of some four thousand Paiutes. As Peleg Brown had written, "If there were a few more people," the settlers would clean them out "root and branch." Now, with the population surge that accompanied the mining boom, there were more. That same population surge squeezed the Indians to a point of desperation where many believed they must fight or starve.

Reports filtered in of Indian troubles farther east along the Humboldt River section of the California Trail, probably involving Shoshone or even Bannocks, who often raided in this area. The Paiute bands had gathered at Pyramid Lake for the annual spring fish run, and the talk was all of war. Chiefs of several bands spoke hotly in favor of war, including Moguanoga (Captain Soo), leader of the Humboldt River band. Moderating voices were few. Truckee, a few months from death, had apparently declined too far into old age to turn the tide one last time; Winnemucca kept silence but was believed to favor war; Indian agent Major Frederick Dodge, often successful in cooling dicey situations, had long been absent in Washington, D.C. One voice, that of Numaga of the Pyramid band, spoke eloquently for peace, warning his people that if they made war, the white men would come like "sand in a whirlwind" and drive them away to starve in the deserts of the North.[8] His convincing words might well have carried the day, as it is clear that the Paiutes had no plan for a general attack and the war talk could have been only a matter of airing grievances and making threats. But a shocking crime took over.

"The road from here to Missouri is infested by a set of scoundrels keeping grog shops by the wayside, most of whom are capable of committing any crime; whose history, if it could be told, would furnish such a tale of horror, that no man could read it without a shudder," Tennessee had written. It was at one of these disreputable grog shops, Williams Station, that two Paiute girls of about twelve who had been digging roots for food were kidnapped, held captive, and molested. The worried parents of the girls traced their tracks to Williams Station but could find no sign of their daughters, and the Williams brothers denied having seen them. Some days later a Paiute trading at the station heard the children's voices. After he brought back this news, a small party led by Moguanoga and including the children's parents and Sarah Winnemucca's brother Natches rode hard for Williams Station. The girls had been concealed in a cellar under the station. On seeing their condition, the enraged Paiutes killed the Williams brothers, along with three men who had been stopping there, and burned the station before returning to Pyramid. A third Williams brother, who had been camping some distance away, later returned to the station, saw the remains, and rode for Virginia City to cry massacre and claim that five hundred Indian warriors had pursued him. As this news spread, it aroused wild excitement and panic. At Pyramid, Numaga, hearing what had happened, said with sorrow, "There is no longer any use for counsel; we must prepare for war."[9]

Many settlers fled over the Sierra Nevada. Ranchers and prospectors from isolated areas made for town; women and children gathered in stone buildings in Virginia City and nearby Silver City. Warned that the Paiutes were coming to plunder and kill, Peleg Brown bundled his sister-in-law Jane and his nieces in an ox-drawn wagon and drove them to Carson. But not all lost their heads. Amid the alarm surrounding him in Genoa, Tennessee observed, "I know there is no more danger of Indians here than there is in San Francisco," and he later cogently noted that if the Paiutes had been launching a general attack they would have struck more sites than Williams Station. He wondered if it might have been useful to inquire into the reason for the attack on this particular site before taking action. Nonetheless, common sense did not prevail among the hotheads, foremost of whom was William Ormsby—"impetuous as a torrent," in the phrase of the *Territorial Enterprise*. What followed was California behavior writ large. After all, had not mobs of miners exterminated entire tribes of Indians in California for any reason or none at all? And many of these men were former Californians. Author John McDermott has concluded that the major failing of whites in the Indian wars was arrogance (to be most famously displayed by George Armstrong Custer at the Little Big Horn).[10] Arrogance ruled that May in 1860, perhaps inflated by the ambition of one man, William Ormsby. If he were to return as the victorious hero of an Indian war, would not his stature as a Nevada leader be restored?

A motley crew of volunteers, poorly equipped and provisioned, set out under the slogan "An Indian for breakfast and a pony to ride" to chastise the "bloodthirsty savages." The volunteers were also poorly led. None but the Carson Rangers would accept Ormsby's leadership. As a result, the men from other communities, Virginia City, Silver City, and Genoa, rode under their own captains, and the force had no unified command. They rode first to Williams Station, where they buried the dead, then headed by stages for Pyramid on the hunt for Indians. Around four in the afternoon of May 12 they spotted a few on the far side of a meadow by the Truckee River and went after them. Too late, in the midst of a deadly cross fire of arrows and bullets, they realized that they had been decoyed into a crescent-shaped ambush.[11]

A disorderly, panic-stricken retreat ensued. Numaga, who had been appointed war chief and calmly directed operations while seated in full regalia on a fine black horse, may have attempted a truce, but his warriors could not be restrained. When the fleeing volunteers retreated to a point near the river, more Indians, led by Sequinata of the Black Rock Desert, burst from concealment in the trees and brush and continued the slaughter. Some volunteers pled in vain for their lives. Ormsby apparently hoped before receiving a fatal bullet that his former Paiute friends would save him. Other volunteers fought heroically. Casting off his heavy Mexican saddle, the desperado Sam Brown pulled the unhorsed lawman John Blackburn up behind him on his prized gray horse Betsy and the two made their getaway. Because Brown was a big, husky man and Blackburn scarcely a pygmy, the star of their narrow escape was undoubtedly Betsy. Men in the demoralized army later said that the most heroic sight they had ever seen was one-legged Captain Richard Watkins on crutches holding the narrow trail up the slope with blazing guns so others could make their escape. Watkins survived.[12]

How many survived and, indeed, how many rode forth expecting an Indian for breakfast and a pony to ride remains fuzzy. After investigating, Judge John Cradlebaugh became convinced that an attack would be unjust and turned back with his men from Williams Station, remarking that Ormsby could shoot his own Indians. In all, the makeshift volunteer army is thought to have numbered 105. The Paiutes later admitted to slaying 46 and said they would have killed every last man if darkness had not intervened. Gradually, men who had hidden in the brush or the river came straggling home over the next several days. It is possible that Paiutes interviewed twenty years afterward in more peaceful times understated the casualties to minimize the damage they had done. Ferol Egan, author of *Sand in a Whirlwind: The Paiute Indian War of 1860,* a book on the war, places the death toll much higher, at 70. If Egan is correct, two-thirds of the volunteer army had perished.[13]

The Pyramid Lake War sent shock waves over the West Coast. First, because by any standard, the death toll was so high. Between 1848 and 1861 only 186 soldiers had been killed in Indian engagements with the army, but in this fight possibly two-thirds of the volunteers had fallen (38 percent of the number of soldiers killed in thirteen years of Indian warfare in the West). Second, this decisive defeat had occurred not at the hands of the mighty Teton Sioux, eighteen thousand strong, nor at those of the aggressive Navaho, three times the number of the Paiutes, but in a battle with a small, obscure Indian tribe that many Californians had never heard of or had despised as "diggers" for their reliance on root foods. Moreover, the battle showed a near reversal of the usual tactical scenario in Indian warfare. Although the Indians generally excelled at ambush, as in the deadly meadow by the Truckee River, superior discipline and teamwork gave the army an edge in a pitched battle. But this mob was not the army, nor did they behave as though they were. The discipline and teamwork instead appeared on the Indian side. This was not the way matters had turned out when mobs sallied forth to annihilate Indians in California.[14]

Had Ormsby survived, he would not have enjoyed hearing his contemporaries roundly condemn the war he had so passionately advocated. Henry DeGroot called it an "Indian War Foolishly Begun and Disastrously Ended." Thomas Knott thought it "useless and unwarranted." William Stewart, the coming power in Nevada politics, found it as "disastrous" as he had predicted. The *Steamer Bulletin's* local correspondent excoriated it: "How humiliating to look back . . . and see what disaster to business, what disgrace to our national character, what wide-spread prejudice to our interests and honor, if not danger to our citizens, are sure to ensue when timid, untruthful and inexperienced men get control of, and give direction to public affairs!"[15]

Although the Pyramid Lake War was an anomaly in several respects, the denouement conformed to the usual pattern: the Indians won the battle but lost the war, as other tribes had done time after time in past engagements and would continue to do for a generation. The Paiutes made no move to follow up the advantage gained by their decisive victory—evidence that they had never intended a general war. The whites, however, determined to recoup their humiliating defeat. Spurred by public demand in both Nevada and California for the "immediate chastisement of the savages," a large force of 207 soldiers and 544 volunteers assembled under the authoritative command of the widely admired former Texas Ranger Jack Hays and marched toward Pyramid rather cautiously, not arriving until June 1. After a scouting party encountered the Paiutes on June 2, Hays decided to advance with about 300 men. Scattered with the rotting bodies of the dead, the terrain was much the same as in the previous battle, mountains to the west, a meadow, and a slope to the Truckee River pleated with gullies. The Paiutes fired from places of concealment, as they had done on May 12, but this time, facing disciplined soldiers and a capable commander, there would be no panicky flight of white volunteers. For much of the afternoon, a mile-long battle line slowly advanced against the Paiutes. Although they met tenacious resistance at every rock and gully, casualties were remarkably light on both sides.[16]

When Hays's force marched into the Pyramid Lake Paiute village two days later, they found it deserted. The Paiutes had fled north into

the Black Rock Desert. Hays and Captain Jasper Stewart, who headed the army unit, concluded that pursuing them into this land of
gleaming white playas and rocky mountains with steep, narrow, and
easily defensible canyons unknown to white men would be useless. Instead, the Paiutes would be starved into submission. Numaga's dark
prophecy had come to pass: "You will be forced among the barren
rocks of the north, where your ponies will die; where you will see
the women and old men starve, and listen to the cries of your children
for food."[17]

Hays and Stewart agreed that the Paiutes had chosen to withdraw
but had not been defeated. For the short run, they disbanded the volunteers a few days later and moved the army to a temporary site, "Fort
Haven," slightly below the lake to prevent the Paiutes from moving
through the pass into the settlements to the south. Indian agent Warren Wasson would supply the Paiutes with provisions to bring them
back to the Pyramid Lake Reservation where they could be controlled.
In mid-July, when the danger seemed passed, the army abandoned
Fort Haven to construct a more permanent post, Fort Churchill, farther south and east of the Comstock on the Carson River.[18]

An uneasy peace prevailed for nearly five years. Many Paiutes,
barely concealing their hostility, returned to Pyramid. White squatters
seized much of the best ranch land belonging to the Indians. After the
1862 murder of eleven emigrants on the Humboldt, the army issued a
harsh order to kill Indian males on sight and "take no prisoners."
Paiute-settler relations reached a crisis point early in 1865 with the
killing of several white men, rightly or wrongly blamed on Indians,
and the infamous Mud Lake Massacre, in which nearly all the women
and children in Winnemucca's unarmed camp lost their lives in an un-
provoked attack by volunteers under army officer Almond Wells. The
savage guerrilla uprising known as the Black Rock War ensued in
1865–1866. Many Paiutes died in fights at Rock Canyon, Fish Creek
Valley, and various smaller skirmishes. A lesser number of soldiers
and settlers also lost their lives before it was over.[19]

Beyond the graves, the Pyramid Lake War had concrete results. Now that the authorities reckoned the Paiutes a dangerous and formidable tribe, the army established two Nevada posts, Fort Churchill near the Carson River and Camp (later Fort) McDermit near the Oregon border. On agent Dodge's 1859 recommendation, the government had also created two reservations for the Paiutes, Pyramid Lake and Walker River, although the executive order finalizing them did not arrive for fifteen years. The Washo, fearful that they might be blamed for the hostilities, declared their peaceful intentions, turned in their arms, and received no reservation. Peace did not pay. Yet after warfare ceased, the policy of peace and adaption championed by Truckee and Winnemucca once more prevailed, and a new generation of Winnemuccas rose to leadership: Winnemucca's son Natches, one day to be elected chief, and his gifted, charismatic daughter Sarah, the eloquent voice of the Paiutes, who would tell the tragic story of her people to large audiences from coast to coast.[20]

Another concrete result of the Pyramid Lake War was immediately felt in the mining business, already reeling from the April stock crash. With the exception of the Ophir and the Gold Hill operations, mining came to a standstill, and those endeavoring to sell their mining stocks could find no takers. An unmistakable signal that mining had nearly halted appeared when fighting over claims also halted. Before the Pyramid Lake War, frontier roughs had received shares in mining claims with the understanding that they would fight for them, and the owners of one mine erected a crude fort for the defense of their property. After the war, a resolution inconceivable to the combatants a few weeks earlier received unanimous approval in Virginia City: "During sixty days, or until the settlement of the present Indian difficulties, no claim or mining ground within the Territory, shall be subject to relocation, or liable to be jumped for non work." Gradually, the dissension and chaos that were the norm revived. Some who had fled to California returned; in July, Tennessee noted a constant stream of wagons and pack mules passing Genoa on its way to Virginia City; and mining production for the year 1860 reached the million-dollar mark, well below early expectations but still promising under the circumstances.[21]

The usual chaos and dissension soon reemerged in politics as well. In his February 1 report to the secretary of state, Utah Territorial governor Alfred Cumming ascribed the "difficulties" in Nevada to "a settled determination on the part of its inhabitants to recognize no courts and obey no laws, except those which have their origin in, and spring directly from primitive assemblages of the people." Yet in the wake of the war, Nevada's primitive assemblages proved unable to decide what form of governance they desired. "Every imaginable kind of organization has been proposed," observed the *Territorial Enterprise*. Some favored a large-scale provisional government, others a return to the vigilance committee. They settled upon an interim solution: a declaration of martial law and a request to Judge John Cradlebaugh, as the only federal official present, to open his court. Under the authority of Captain Johns, a former soldier, guards patrolled Virginia City nightly and the residents put up a fort. Presumably, these measures lapsed when it became clear that no danger from Indians threatened.[22]

In addition to the unresolved issues of governance, disputes over offices presently broke out. Judge Cradlebaugh willingly convened his court in Carson City on June 11, but the presidential appointment of a new judge for the district, Robert Flenniken, a former minister to The Hague, undermined his authority. After the elderly Flenniken, with a pompous air and a fine silk hat said to be the only one of its kind in the territory, arrived, Cradlebaugh refused to relinquish his office on the grounds that federal judges could not be removed except by congressional action. Although territorial judges were subject to summary removal by presidents, the matter would be settled in Cradlebaugh's favor by the Utah Territorial Supreme Court in 1861.[23]

After probate judge John Child called an election for several vacant local offices on August 6, a dispute flared over the office of recorder, always a lucrative position in mining country because entering claims earned the recorder about fifty dollars a day. Although Judge Child had not declared a vacancy in the office held by Stephen Kinsey, several eager candidates offered themselves, and Edward Morse believed that he had been elected. R. M. Anderson, a member of the committee appointed to tally the ballots, asked to count the vote for recorder. When Judge Child refused to allow it, Anderson responded that the judge deserved to be hanged. Henry Lufkin, a brother-in-law of the judge, then commenced a gunfight with Anderson, who was shot in the chest but recovered. After Morse set himself up as the recorder in an office, the miners, unsure who was the legal recorder and unwilling to take chances, entered their claims with both recorders. Disputed elections were fast becoming a Nevada tradition, and this contest would not be resolved until a third party was appointed to the post the following year.[24]

Though local political developments were hardly encouraging, on the national level they were even worse. As would often prove true in Nevada's history, far-away events had greater impact that anything occurring on the spot. This time the ominous shadow of the approaching Civil War, Republican policy for organizing the West, and events in the Dakotas reverberated in Nevada. In one of the more bizarre twists of political life, the southerner William Smith, chairman of the House Committee on Territories and Nevada Territory's former advocate, had been replaced by radical Republican congressman Galusha Grow of Pennsylvania, the new champion of Nevada and the other proposed territories. After the James Crane's death, his friend Smith had evidently abandoned the hope that Nevada would become a slave state; in a complete reversal, he would vote against the Nevada bill he had formerly championed with effusive oratory and would presently depart to serve in the Confederate Congress. Grow was his opposite. A tall thirty-five year old with glossy black hair and beard and sharp, fierce black eyes, Grow lost no opportunity to harass southerners in Congress. During the debate over Kansas, he grappled on the floor of Congress with a southerner who had called him a "black Republican puppy," to which Grow responded that no southern slave driver could crack the whip over his back. The brawl escalated into a general melee. Ironically, on May 11, the day before the Pyramid Lake War, Galusha Grow reported a bill creating three new territories, Dakota, Nevada, and Colorado, from the newly Republican-controlled House Committee on Territories. The Nevada and Colorado bills were immediately tabled, with Dakota soon to follow, after a rousing speech by Iowa congressman Samuel Curtis who favored organizing the lawless West and suspected a plot to open the West to railroad land grants.[25]

Although southern congressmen opposed it, the issue was not dead because the Republican drive to control the West and prevent the spread of slavery was gathering force. As historian Howard Lamar points out, Republican support of a homestead law (warmly sponsored by Galusha Grow) necessitated new territories where farmers could settle—and, not incidentally, vote Republican. Also, organized territories would open the door to transcontinental land grants and provide the newly elected Republican administration with bountiful opportunities for patronage. In addition to his militancy, Grow became known as the father of the 1862 Homestead Act. For this bill he needed a solid Republican base to be secured through the western territories where the concept of "free homes for free men" enjoyed great popularity. Therefore, Grow energetically promoted the territories, and Nevada, though largely unsuited to agriculture, benefited from his dedication to the Homestead Act.

In December Massachusetts congressman Eli Thayer attempted an end run around the House Committee on Public Lands and reported a bill to create a "Dakota Land District" that would have meant Democratic control of the area. Much now depended on Congressman Grow. To counter Thayer's Dakota bill, Grow proposed organizing the entire remainder of the West into five territories, including Nevada. Thayer then maneuvered his Dakota bill to the Committee of the Whole instead of the Committee on Territories. The bill died there, but Grow's comprehensive plan did not advance either. Assiduous lobbying by

John Musser (Crane's replacement), repeated petitions from the residents, and perhaps news of the exciting discoveries on the Comstock had kept Nevada on the agenda. In the spring, J. Ross Browne had noticed a building boom by Carson City boosters anticipating that their town would be the new territorial capital.[26] They were only slightly premature.

Such a Motley Crowd: The 1860 Census

HE YEAR 1860 may have been the worst possible for an accurate count of the Nevada population. Not only had the war ignited an exodus followed by a backflow, but also, in the phrase of historian Ronald James, "society was in continuous flux," the usual situation in the early stages of a mining boom. All the same, 1860 was the year of the first Nevada census, providing a rough image of the size and character of the population nine years after settlement began. Though not numerous, the newcomers showed the components of a fledgling society, no longer merely a handful of prospectors, ranchers, and traders. Consciously, many expected territorial status; the building boom in Carson City, the likely capital, suggested as much. Unconsciously, the newcomers' rush of 1860 set a pattern of boomtown culture that has defined Nevada for most of its existence.

The census reported a population of 6,857 (not including Indians), a small figure but a sharp rise over earlier years. In February Governor Alfred Cumming, no doubt on scanty information, had estimated the non-Mormon population (mainly in Nevada) at two thousand to three thousand This roughly conformed to Tennessee's guess of one thousand in the Carson Valley, perhaps one-third to one-half the total. Nonetheless, these numbers suggest the small size of the population before the spring rush. The Comstock stimulated exploration in the outlying regions, and it is doubtful that the census included all of these, especially where boundaries had not yet gelled. Interest in the

Walker River diggings had revived; mining had commenced in "Esmeralda" (the future Aurora), among other new sites; and late in the year hopeful miners reopened the Potosi Mine southwest of Las Vegas, then inside New Mexico territory and thus not part of the count.[1]

In place of the seasonal scattering of gold washers with rockers in Gold Canyon, the elements of a permanent industrial workforce had appeared. In the mining towns of Virginia City and Gold Hill, more than 70 percent of the workforce were miners. These men labored under difficult and dangerous conditions because the unstable clays of these mountains readily swelled and buckled the inadequate supports erected inside the tunnels. Death in cave-ins continually threatened. Fortunately for future operations on the Comstock, the new arrivals in November included Philipp Deidesheimer, a young German-born mining engineer who had graduated from the prestigious Freiburg School of Mines and gained practical experience for ten years in the California gold country. After brief study of the problem, Deidesheimer devised the famous square-set timbering system of strong open boxes that could be fitted together both horizontally and vertically. First erected in the Ophir, his system soon spread throughout the Comstock and before long became used and admired throughout the mining world. Regrettably, Deidesheimer had not patented his invention and thus reaped no financial rewards from its widespread popularity, but he could draw satisfaction from the many miners' lives he had saved.[2]

Even though the Comstock had not triggered the same degree of national and international excitement as the California gold rush, Deidesheimer's German origins reflect the fact that a higher proportion (30 percent) of foreign-born residents than most other states would distinguish the Nevada populace for years to come. The Irish formed the largest single ethnic group on the Comstock, followed by the Germans. Hispanics also appeared prominently on the census. Most were packers—those cursing vaqueros whose fast-paced mule trains jingling with bells had sent J. Ross Browne scrambling on the

The square-set timbering system invented by Philipp Deidesheimer saved many miners' lives on the Comstock and throughout the world. From Dan De Quille, *The Big Bonanza*, p. 93.

Sierra Nevada trails—but Hispanics also became successful mining entrepreneurs. Using archaic methods that dated from sixteenth-century Spanish practices, the Maldonado brothers turned the Mexican Mine into one of the most successful early producers.[3]

Occupation tends to be a more slippery category than national origins, as J. R. "Poker" Brown, who ranched for the summers and mined in the winters, had demonstrated, and most on the census taker's list depended directly or indirectly on the Comstock mines. In the spring journalist Browne found Virginia City "infested with gentlemen of the bar, thirsting and hungering for chances at the Comstock. If it could only be brought into court, what a picking of bones there would be!" They must have considered the pickings rather lean in the wake of the war, for the business directory listed only five lawyers, all in Carson City where Judge Cradlebaugh held court, and the census taker counted several more (apparently not practicing) on the Comstock. Doctors (nineteen) scattered through the various communities outnumbered the legal fraternity and ministered to the pressing needs of those like Browne who developed a "complication of miseries" under the primitive living conditions. In addition to the usual range of construction and service workers and tradespeople, jewelers and confectioners offered luxuries in a place where it had recently been impossible to buy a pair of boots. One wonders how the "gritty cusses" brought in to fight for claims and the congregating desperados defined their occupations to the census taker.[4]

Unlike the politicians who lusted to become governor or a congressional delegate, for these habitués of the Comstock saloons the height of ambition was the august and unofficial title of big chief of the Comstock. Although the cool, gentlemanly Langford Peel and others had their admirers, the desperado who came closest to achieving this dubious distinction in the early days was Sam Brown. Yes, Sam was back after several guards and the judge who convicted him petitioned for his release from San Quentin. And he was much the same, still a large, flamboyant, red-haired figure with jangling Mexican spurs, still a pleasant fellow when sober and a demon when drunk. Since his return in 1859, his roster of killings had increased by two, one of them probably justified.[5]

As Sam loomed large among the aspiring big chiefs, Sheriff John Blackburn gained an equally commanding position among early Nevada lawmen and presided over a district soon to be enlarged to seventy thousand square miles, most of them uninhabited. The image of the two of them riding the same horse as they fled the war together seems appropriate because in several ways they were mirror images. Both were California gamblers who moved on to Nevada; both were young men in their twenties with romantic involvements (Blackburn had a wife and Brown a married mistress in the Carson Valley); both had business interests on the side in mining claims and real estate. Both killed on little provocation: Brown's victims reached a confirmed minimum of five and a probable total of eight; during drinking bouts, Blackburn killed a man who cursed him and allegedly another who sang too boisterously. Indeed, the sheriff began to consider himself above the law and fast approached the common description of Brown as a demon when drunk. As this suggests, the line between lawman and desperado often blurred on the frontier, and some appeared in both occupations at different times. Both Sam Brown and John Blackburn were to die violently the following year in quarrels that could have been avoided.[6]

Of "gritty cusses" there were altogether too many, of lawmen an increasing number—Blackburn hired nine deputies—and of women never enough, ever since the days when Peleg Brown bewailed the absence of "socety." Slightly more than one-tenth of the population were women, a figure nearly as low as in the California gold rush days of 1850, and Carson City contained the largest concentration of them (167). This may indicate that in the aspiring capital, anticipation of territorial status and liberation from Mormon rule made men more likely to bring their wives and put down roots. Better than half the women dwelled in Carson and in the old ranching and trading communities. As in California's days of gold, some of the smaller mining districts, such as Palmyra and Flowery, had no women at all. In the mining towns, the search for bonanza was the order of the day, and saloon culture was the way of life. Wives, homes, and churches lagged far behind. In December 1860 Augustin Hale, a pious New Englander who sorely missed attending church with his family, walked five miles to Virginia City where he heard there would be preaching—only to be disappointed when none took place. In 1862 Hale reported little improvement in Gold Hill. The itinerant Methodist preacher had suspended his visits after the citizenry declared themselves too poor to raise funds to build a meeting house. Hale sarcastically observed that they found no difficulty in raising eighteen hundred dollars for a grand ball.[7]

Though more common than preachers, women remained rare enough to be noticed; journalist Browne commented on the women he saw in the rush over the Sierra Nevada wearing men's clothes and riding mules. It is mainly through the eyes of others that we see them, because that mother lode for historians, diaries and letters, is largely lacking in this early period. The prostitute Julia Bulette, better known in our day than hers, arrived several years later, as did most prostitutes. Historian Ronald James has observed that in the early period, wives far outnumbered the storied soiled doves with hearts of gold. (Instead of a heart of gold, Bulette reputedly sported a volunteer fireman's badge presented to her in recognition of her services to the company; her grave site is now concealed, lest vandals rip the badge from her corpse.)[8]

One of the main women to be remembered from early Comstock days was Scotch-born Alleson ("Eilley") Orrum, a Mormon. At fifteen she married Stephen Hunt, whom she divorced in Utah when he took a second wife. She then married another Mormon, Alexander Cowan, in 1853. The Cowans came with the 1855 Mormon contingent to Nevada, where they lived together until he permanently deserted her in

1858. To support herself, Eilley ran a boardinghouse for the Gold Canyon miners and worked as a washerwoman. After divorcing Cowan in 1860, Eilley married prospector Sandy Bowers, a simple, illiterate Scot. Each owned ten feet of a small claim at Gold Hill that turned out to be rich enough to make them wealthy. They built an expensive mansion in Washoe Valley (which still stands today as a public resort) and embarked on an extensive three-year tour of Europe, extravagances that diminished their fortune. Following their return, Sandy died, and the mismanagement of a dishonest superintendent left Eilley destitute and telling fortunes for a living in her old age. The enduring interest of her story lies in its rags-to-riches and back-to-rags trajectory.[9]

Two powerful women from the early period were not victims like Eilley—anything but—or beneficiaries of luck. They created their own roles and speak to us in their own words. Bloomer girl, suffragette, and feminist Hannah Keziah Clapp was a woman of strong opinions and indomitable will. Before traveling to California by wagon train with her brother and his family in 1859, she had served as principal of a female seminary in Michigan, among other teaching positions. For a while she taught in California before plumping herself down in Carson City in 1860 at age thirty-six to organize a school with the same determination she had shown when she marched into a Salt Lake City Mormon service wearing bloomers and packing a revolver. Hannah Keziah made no idle plans, and what she planned was not a small operation in a pioneer living room but a sizable private coeducational school with space for forty boarders as well as day pupils. Her Sierra Seminary soon rose and remained a principal feature of the Nevada educational scene until 1887, when she left for Reno following financial reversals to become a professor at the new University of Nevada. By the time of her death in 1908, this pioneer educator had left a legacy no less important than Eilley's mansion.[10]

The one who stood foremost among Nevada women in this or any other time was Sarah Winnemucca, the voice of the Paiutes. In 1860

Pioneer educator Hannah Clapp had been known
to wear bloomers and pack a gun. Courtesy Nevada
Historical Society, Reno.

Sarah was only sixteen, and her many accomplishments lay ahead.
Fluent in English, among several languages, she would interpret and
mediate between Paiutes and whites; she would volunteer as a scout
for the army in the Bannock War; she would travel to Washington,
D.C., to plead the Paiute cause before high officials; in lectures on both
coasts, her emotional speeches on Paiute grievances would move large
audiences; she would found a model school that showed how Indian
children could be taught with kindness and respect for their culture;
and, perhaps most significantly, she would write a book, *Life among*

the Piutes: Their Wrongs and Claims (1883), the first by an Indian woman and the first by any Indian west of the Rockies. It is this book, above all, that assumes importance in the 1851–1861 period because not only does she preserve in its pages the increasingly threatened heritage of her people but she also relates the events of that time from a Paiute point of view.[11]

Remarkable figures like Sarah Winnemucca and Hannah Keziah Clapp do not, however, tell us enough about the lives of ordinary women on the Nevada frontier. Historian Ronald James has determined that most on the Comstock were young women between twenty and thirty-five. The presence of these young wives shows the trend toward a real community where people had some expectation of remaining. An occasional glimpse of women's lives also appears in the probate court records of nine divorces in the 1855–1861 period. Women sought all but one. The impossibility of a reconciliation was a theme repeated in virtually all the divorces because the complaints had been shaped to the grounds allowed by law (a point sometimes missed in studies of divorce). Being still under Utah law, Nevada divorces conformed to Brigham Young's view that divorce should be readily granted not only on the usual grounds such as desertion and adultery but also when the parties had no affection for each other, found themselves incompatible, and averred that they could not be reconciled.[12]

Most women also mentioned desertion, raising the image of irresponsible frontier husbands vamoosing in pursuit of a new will-o'-the-wisp. Although no complaint charged adultery, this does not necessarily mean that none occurred. Tennessee reported at the fall 1859 session of the district court that "the most notorious murderers were allowed to pass unnoticed" while men and women indicted for adultery "engrossed the undivided attention of the Grand Jury." The difference probably lies in the source of the complaint. Outside parties would bring violations of community morality to the grand jury's attention; individuals seeking a divorce would prefer to avoid scandal and shape their cases on less shocking grounds, a growing trend in the nineteenth century. A curious anecdote related by Browne suggests the presence of community mores on marital matters: when stage drivers warned an innkeeper that he should formally marry the mother of his children or face vigilante action, the man hastily complied. This threat may have been a joke, but the innkeeper found it plausible.[13]

All divorces were granted without contest. Women received the custody of the children in every instance, but they gained no alimony or support excepting a "piece of land" for Eilley Orrum and prior arrangements in two cases. The avowal that she supports herself "by labor" recurs in the instances of deserted wives. Just what that meant was evident in Eilley Orrum's arduous (albeit well-paid) drudgery at the washtub and Thomas Knott's recollection of a hardworking young woman on a Carson Valley ranch: "Got up at 5 in the morning, and went to bed at eight at night, skimmed 60 to 70 pans of milk a day, fed 14 to 15 men a day during hay time, and kept the house clean for $25.00 a month." When these divorces were granted, the judge pronounced his verdict with a finality that resounded like the crack of doom: "The bonds of matrimony heretofore existing [shall] be fully and completely disolved as tho the said defendant was naturally dead."[14]

With the exception of Eilley Orrum, the denouement for the women who briefly appear in these divorce suits is not known. Because women were scarce and in great demand, they may have remarried as speedily as she did. After all, frontier women had already shown themselves open to new beginnings by joining the western adventure. The moral milieu in which these women lived may have been shifting. Hints that marital behavior had recently been rather elastic surface in the stories of Lucky Bill's mistress, Martha Lamb, and Sam Brown's married mistress, but that stage delineated by historian Nancy Taniguchi in which Yankee women arrived after the California gold rush and imposed their version of Victorian morality apparently clamped down fairly early. A leading historian argues that although the Comstock was a "man's world," the towns soon became Victorian in dress

and manners and wives were held in "chivalrous regard." No one recounted an off-color joke in the theater or the press. Polygamy had
long been opposed by Nevadans on moral grounds as one of their
objections to Mormon rule, and those adultery indictments by the
grand jury also indicate a strict sense of public morality. All the same,
the frontier flavor still occasionally appeared in women's behavior in
1860. When Mrs. Heiss, a German emigrant, shot and killed a His-
panic in the courtroom where his bail had just been set for making ad-
vances to her, followed by threats, the spectators in the packed courtroom burst into tumultuous applause—much to the disgust of Judge
John Cradlebaugh.[15]

Settlers in the valleys no longer dominated politically and economically, and the valleys were fast becoming dependents of the Comstock,
a ready market for all the ranchers could produce. Now the Comstock
was where the action was. Yet even though men of the Comstock like
William Stewart had replaced William Ormsby and his kind and big
chiefs and gritty cusses on the Comstock had replaced rural vigilantes,
the valleys also thrived and grew. Old groups returned and new ones
arrived. Under the protection of the U.S. Army, now ensconced in Utah
at Camp Floyd, perhaps as many as two hundred apostates fearing
death at Mormon hands had departed in 1859. They probably went on
to California, but in the summer of 1860 Tennessee noted the arrival of
many Utah Mormons, some of them apostates. While these 1860 settlers may have signaled continuing dissidence in the church, they did
not represent an attempt by Brigham Young to "secure, secure" the
western edge of his kingdom, an idea he had long since renounced.
Rather, just as the early Mormon traders had responded to the economic opportunities of the great emigration, these 1860 arrivals knew
that a mining boom spelled prosperity for nearby ranchers.[16]

It was not the Mormons, however, but an influx of arrivals from
Germany who would eventually predominate in the Carson Valley.
Many came from Westphalia, following Old Dutch Fred Dangberg's
optimistic letters in the daisy-chain pattern often characteristic of

emigration. But not all. August Dressler followed a different path, first farming in New York, then homesteading in Minnesota, where he found it too cold—cold enough, he told his grandson, "to freeze the horns off the cows." Having heard of California gold, he set off with a partner on a six-month trek by ox team to a better place. Even in 1860, eleven years after the California gold rush, the journey was not an easy one, and his throat became so parched when crossing the Forty Mile Desert that he stooped down to drink rainwater from the wagon ruts. Finding the Carson Valley a thriving place, he dropped his California idea and eventually settled in the southeastern part of the valley. An earlier rancher had abandoned the place because of its numerous mountain lions. Neither unearthly yowls nor the menace of swift-moving, buff-colored predators fazed the Dresslers, and their descendants still live there today, even after so many of the old families have left their lands.[17]

The influx of newcomers in the Truckee Meadows meant more conviviality for Peleg Brown, no more to be "loathsome at times." Some of the merrymaking in which he participated was related as follows:

> The boys of these days were a jolly crew, and if there was any amusement going on they wanted a share. . . . Hearing there would be a dance at the springs, about twenty got together and determined to have one dance at least. When they arrived at the festive scene they found that George Lamroux was the only man in the crowd who had a "biled" shirt. . . . They came to the conclusion that they were not presentable in their colored garments, and, in order to let each one have a swing, George must pass the shirt around. George went in and had a dance, and while he was gone the rest drew lots for turns. By the time every one of them had worn the garment and had a dance, the shirt was black as a crow.[18]

In the fall of 1860 Peleg made his long-postponed visit to Rhode Island and learned where he really belonged. As his mother delicately put it, he had been "quite naturalized"—turned into a westerner. Joshua, minding the ranch in Peleg's absence, never became naturalized. Perhaps still debilitated from the long illness that kept him on the edge of the Plains, he wrote of feeling his age (thirty-two), wanting to sell the ranch, and finding himself "much drove." He did not glory in the sunny winter days, the financial opportunities, or the hours spent in the saddle like a real westerner, as Peleg had done. It was a country for the young and the energetic. Joshua would soon move back to Rhode Island with his wife and children; Peleg returned to spend the rest of his life in the "finest plaice in the valley." He would marry, no more to miss the "socety" of women, and father several children. And he would die in 1878 of heart disease at age forty-two, a respected and successful pioneer mourned as a "good square man."[19]

Territory! 1861

HE CRITICAL MONTHS from January to March 1861 are a black hole in Nevada's local history. No copies of the *Territorial Enterprise* have been preserved for these dates, and the *Mountain Democrat* has little to say. The writers of letters, memoirs, and diaries are silent. The ironic and informative dispatches of Tennessee have ceased; he will die in eastern Nevada in an unnecessary 1870 dispute over a bill resulting in a shootout, which he acknowledged was his own fault. Yet, it could be argued that this void in local sources from the Sierra Nevada to Salt Lake City mattered little because the main events affecting Nevada happened far away, in Washington, D.C.[1]

In the winter of 1860–1861, Nevada floated like a cork on the rushing tide of momentous national events. Abraham Lincoln had been elected president with only 39.9 percent of the vote in a divided field; lacking a mandate, he maintained a low profile during the interregnum between the November election and his inauguration on March 4, 1861. The congressional Republicans lacked both leadership and experience in the role of a majority party. Further, they were in denial, unable to believe that the Southerners, who had so often threatened secession, really meant it this time. Even after the Deep South, beginning with South Carolina in December, had deserted the Union, the president elect and many in his party continued to believe that with a policy of patience and conciliation the South would reenter the Union without war. As the wily and resourceful William Seward, Lincoln's secretary of state designate, assumed command of the congressional Republicans, placating the border states, including Virginia and Kentucky, in hopes that they would forego secession became a primary aim and greater cooperation with Democrats a means. For the newly and unsteadily ascendant Republicans, organizing the West looked more feasible than it had been in 1860 because the secession of the South had eliminated the deadlock over slavery in the territories that had stymied action for years. Also, in the midst of the secession crisis, strengthening the bond between the western regions and the Union had grown more necessary than ever. When Senator James Green of Missouri, a strong proslavery Democrat, introduced bills on February 15, 1861, creating the territories of Nevada and Dakota, Seward and the militant Republican congressional leader Galusha Grow supported them.[2]

The mighty controversy over slavery in the territories that had split the nation did not die without a final struggle, however. In late February an amendment dealing with slavery became a point of contention in the territorial bills. Grow, and other leading Republicans, reached an agreement at conferences with Green to drop the slavery issue. The deciding battle on the territorial bills erupted in the House on March 1, 1861, during the dying days of the lame-duck session of the Congress elected in 1858. In a scene described by historian Howard Lamar as one of "great confusion, cries of order, motions for adjournment," and other disruptions, Grow presented the Nevada bill at breakneck speed, mentioning that no slavery clause was included, and it passed ninety-five to fifty-two. The Dakota measure also whipped through, and President Buchanan signed the territorial bills, with Colorado as well, on March 2, just two days before Lincoln took office.[3]

It was, and is, cause for considerable astonishment that the Republicans who had fought so fiercely for the exclusion of slavery from the western territories had abandoned it at the eleventh hour. In essence, if not in name, they had endorsed "popular sovereignty," the concept

Pennsylvania congressman Galusha Grow, a "black
Republican puppy" to his political enemies, steered
the bills creating new western territories through
Congress. Courtesy Library of Congress, Washington, D.C.

that the voters of a territory should decide for themselves to be free or
slave. This was an idea that militant antislavery politicians had opposed when Senator Stephen Douglas advocated it during the Kansas-
Nebraska controversy in 1854—an irony recognized by Douglas. The
reason for the Republican reversal appears to have been their policy of
conciliation toward the South, coupled with a growing belief that as a
practical matter slavery could never take root in these territories. They
were also well aware that with appointed Republican officials locally
in charge in the new territories, Republican policies would prevail.
Other reasons for the Republican drive in 1860 to organize the terri-

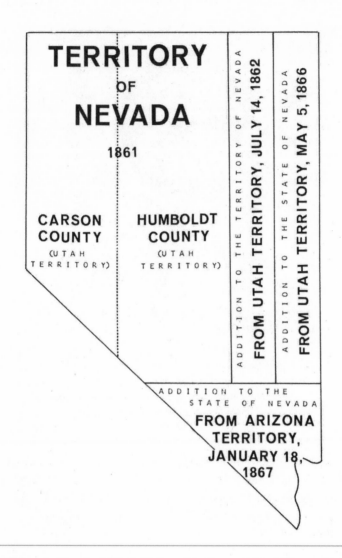

Additions to Nevada, 1862–1867. From John Koontz, *Political History of Nevada*, *1965*, p. 99.

tories seemed equally pressing: the settlement of farmers under the forthcoming Homestead Act (Grow's pet policy), transcontinental land grants for railroad construction, and patronage for the host of office seekers beating on the doors of the new administration. Stripped of any mention of slavery, the territorial bills had passed, but the South had moved beyond conciliation. Weeks later, on April 12, they fired on Fort Sumter.[4]

The question remains: "Why Nevada?" After all, despite continual objections by the settlers, the region had been organized, in some fashion, by Utah and just reorganized in January 1861. Lawlessness still prevailed, as it had in 1860 when a San Francisco newspaper observed: "Politically, the people are in a chaotic state without law. . . . The evils to which they are exposed are terrible to contemplate and the coming season it is to be feared, will witness scenes of anarchy and bloodshed, fearful to behold, as the rich silver mines will attract thither a large crowd of desperate and abandoned men." No matter. Political conditions in Nevada seem to have played little part in Republican thinking, and they probably cared nothing about the assertions of earlier Nevada petitioners on 250 fertile valleys and vast hordes of menacing Indians. What mattered was not what territorial status would do for Nevada but what Nevada would do for the Union. The population was ridiculously small compared to other territories. No matter. Galusha Grow, the territory's new champion, had already declared in the contest over the Kansas and Oregon bill in 1859 that the size of the population made no difference. With the rush to the Comstock still in full swing, congressmen who thought about the matter at all may have supposed that another event comparable to the California gold rush had erupted and the population would rapidly balloon.[5]

What territory Nevada contained was still very foggy. The Honey Lake Valley? No, California's as of 1864–1865. The Las Vegas region, a recent addition to Arizona Territory? Yes, later given to Nevada in 1867. The eastern deserts? Yes, two large swaths added to Nevada at Utah's expense in 1862 and 1866. Aurora, then the scene of mining excitement not far behind the Comstock? Ultimately yes, the result of a surveyor's conclusion, although for a while the town had two governments, Nevada's and California's, and the residents voted in both. No matter. Nevada may have been an ill-defined blob on the map, but it contained the Comstock. Expansion on the ground accompanied this expansion on the map as Nevadans rapidly colonized the formidable Great Basin over the following decade at a series of new mining sites until the vast emptiness formerly traversed by just a few emigrant trails showed a spiderweb of trails and turnpikes. As historian Eugene Moehring observes, rapid control of the region was a matter of no small importance because it "secured this strategic land bridge connecting California with the rest of the nation."[6]

Lincoln himself, in a letter to Schuyler Colfax several years later reflecting views he had likely held for some time, wrote of the social and financial importance of the western mines: "I have very large ideas of the mineral wealth of our Nation. . . . It abounds all over the western country . . . and its development has scarcely commenced." Lincoln went on to say that he saw mining not only as a source of specie that would help to pay the national debt but also as an occupational safety valve providing employment for both arriving immigrants and veterans with "room enough for all." One thing only mattered—the Comstock. This showed clearly in Grow's 1860 territorial bill, in which the future Nevada appeared as "Washoe Silver Mines." Hubert Howe Bancroft's history states the situation unequivocally: "The state of Nevada came into being through the discovery and development of the Comstock lode."[7]

Whether the congressmen who pressed for a Nevada territory realized it or not, the bond between Nevada and the Union much needed cementing. Some, but not all, Nevadans reacted to the defection of the South with fierce patriotism. Writing to his mother in February 1861, Augustin Hale reported that the region had been little affected by the "great disunion movements" but the people "look with *Horror* & *disgust* upon the treachery of the South, & under *any* & *all* circumstances will always be found with their brethren of the *North*. Ninety nine out of every hundred who speak on the subject, express the wish that South Carolina might be sunk in the bottom of the Ocean." He greatly underestimated the strength of secessionist sentiment in Nevada. During 1861 the Confederates' ambitious plans to conquer the West seemed well on the way to realization. A force of Texans took Arizona and parts of southern New Mexico. The larger aim was the conquest of the Mexican states of Sonora and Chihuahua, southern California, where many Confederate sympathizers had concentrated, then "on to San Francisco" and the remainder of the West. The potential benefits to the Confederacy looked enormous: Pacific ports, the wealth of the western mines (no doubt including Nevada's), more men and supplies, and, possibly, European recognition.[8]

More than a few Nevadans looked on these early Confederate victories in the Southwest with favor, and the arrival of Nevada's first territorial governor, James Nye, in mid-July 1861, and with him the rudiments of a Union territorial government, failed to quash their hopes. The belief that many Nevadans harbored Southern sympathies and Nevada had potential as a future slave state had probably helped James Crane to persuade the Virginia congressman William Smith to champion the Nevada territorial bill several years earlier. Although no hard figures are available, the newspaperman and historian Sam Davis thought Nevada contained a larger proportion of Southern sympathizers than any other part of the Far West, perhaps equal in numbers to the Union men. Moreover, the secessionists were a militant and vocal crew, and early Confederate victories on the battlefield made them cocky. "At every rebel success," wrote Davis, "one might easily have imagined himself in the victorious rebel camp, so loud was the rejoicing." This jubilation overflowed in the saloons where the gamblers congregated. They were believed to be secessionist, and certainly that was true of Sam Brown, soon to be shot by an enemy he had threatened as he paused to water his horse on the way to join the Confederate army. In June 1861, within four months of the passage of the

territorial bill, the commander of the Department of the Pacific increased the number of troops at Fort Churchill to counter the secessionist threat.[9]

The Comstock celebrated the Fourth of July 1861 with a fervid dis-
play of loyalty to the Union. Large American flags flew, 2,500 people
paraded through the streets, a band played, cannons fired, patriotic
oratory flowed, and fireworks lit the night. But neither cannons nor
oratory could drown rebel intransigence. Sometime afterward an up-
roar broke out when a rebel raised a Confederate flag over a Virginia
City building and stood by with several men to protect it. His business
partner, not sharing his views, hoisted a Union flag at the other end of
the building and announced he would shoot anyone who tried to re-
move it. For several hours the excitement in the street threatened to
erupt into open warfare, but finally the Confederate flag was taken
down, never to fly again in Virginia City. In addition to this near riot,
the Nevada rebels pursued what the *Silver Age* out of Carson City
called a "cunning policy" of creating dissension among Union supporters as the new territory unsteadily approached its first legislative
election. Like most political groupings, the Union men incorporated a
varied range of opinions, and the rebels cleverly played upon their
differences. By styling the Civil War "Abe Lincoln's War" or the "un-
constitutional war," they strove to divide the Union movement and
elect their own men. In this they failed. Though it may have been a
near thing, Union men dominated the election.[10]

By the summer of 1862, Colorado volunteers and U.S. troops had
driven the Confederates out of the Southwest and southern California
had been placed under virtual martial law, but the Nevada rebels remained unsubdued. In August 1862 the new commander at Fort
Churchill, Colonel P. Edward Connor, found it necessary to order all
subordinate commanders to arrest and closely confine any persons
"uttering sentiments against the Government" until they took the oath
of allegiance. Connor concluded: "Traitors shall not utter treasonable
sentiments in this district with impunity . . . or receive the punishment

[162]

they so richly merit." Before the end of the month rebels in Aurora put his order to the test on a Saturday night by making a "complete pandemonium" of the town and taunting an army officer with cheers for Jeff Davis. They no doubt were well aware that the officer's troops had been stationed elsewhere. The volunteer Esmeralda rifles rallied to the occasion, however. They imprisoned the rebel leader, distributed arms to their supporters, countered rebel threats to take the armory, and saw the oath administered to their less rambunctious prisoner on Sunday morning.[11]

Although the identity of all but the most vocal of these Southern sympathizers in Nevada remained unclear, a few personalities stand out. One of these was undoubtedly the lawyer and former Texas Ranger David Terry, a long-haired, heavy-set, six footer with a bulbous nose and, less obviously, a concealed bowie knife. Like many in the California backwash, he came to Nevada under a cloud, having killed California U.S. senator David Broderick in a duel in 1859. Onlookers anticipated a battle of the titans when Terry and William Stewart squared off in a mining lawsuit, the Ophir Mine represented by Stewart versus McCall and the "middle lead" boys represented by Terry. I. P. Corrigan, an unsympathetic observer, thought McCall "the lowest scum" and expressed shock that a man with an "elegant family" in California like Terry could be seen anytime arm in arm with McCall "drinking and frequenting the lowest places in town." When Judge John Cradlebaugh opened court over a livery stable in Genoa in the fall of 1860, a host of three or four hundred armed men crowded into the room and overflowed Genoa's accommodations. The judge was obliged to sleep between rival attorneys on a mound of straw in the barn. Many expected a gun battle in the courtroom at any moment, and, indeed, shots had been fired at witnesses as they rode hard down Gold Canyon. Corrigan saw Genoa as "a place full of inequities where we have small chance of a righteous jury or justice of any kind." He added, "My *private* opi[nion] is that there will be a tragedy in the affair before it leaves the court." These dark forebodings proved unfounded.

David Terry, a lawyer, duelist, and secessionist leader in Nevada and California.
Courtesy Nevada Historical Society, Reno.

No shootout erupted in the courtroom, attorneys avoided inflamma-
tory remarks, Terry made no attempt to browbeat witnesses, and the
intimidated jury found themselves unable to reach a verdict. The battle of the titans had ended inconclusively.[12]

Because Terry was the foremost rebel leader in Nevada, his fortunes
resonated beyond the immediate legal issues he argued in court. He
underwent a more definitive legal defeat when he made the mistake of
relying upon that weak reed Judge Robert Flenniken, which enabled
William Stewart to outfox him in the interpretation of mining law and
in his attempt to hold the disputed mines. His legal career in Nevada

[164]

failed to prosper, a setback to rebel hopes, and for several years he divided his time between Nevada and California, where his wife and children resided. Army communications make clear that some believed he led the Nevada secessionists and extended his treasonous plans to southern California. Although the wilder tales about Terry's secessionist activities have never been proved, suspicions of his leadership in a subterranean movement lasted until his 1863 departure, by secret ways, to join the Confederate army.[13]

Dr. Selden McMeans was a fellow southerner and a like-minded friend of Terry's since their days as California politicians together. In the mood for adventure at age fifty-three, he moved to Virginia City in 1859 to practice medicine and soon put his Southern sympathies into practice to support the Confederacy. With Terry, he organized a local chapter perhaps two hundred strong of the Knights of the Golden Circle, a secret society of an estimated sixty-five thousand southerners. The Golden Circle meant Mexico and Central America divided into slave states and incorporated in the Confederacy, a nightmare to Union men because it signified a revival of the ambitious fantasies of William Walker and other filibusterers. Energized by the firing on Fort Sumter, McMeans openly declared that the rebels would capture Fort Churchill and take the territory for the South. Nonetheless, the Knights made no aggressive moves. Before the end of the war, McMeans took a more moderate path and led in organizing the Democratic Party in Nevada, where he continued to practice medicine until his death in 1876.[14]

There may have been some uncertainty about Terry's activities, McMeans may have put a moderate face on his Southern sympathies, but Patrick Henry (Hal) Clayton's "treasonable expressions," to which he gave voice on every occasion, left no room for doubt. The press called him a "howling secessionist." A brilliant lawyer, bon vivant, reckless gambler, heavy drinker (until he took the pledge), and cockfighting enthusiast, Clayton exuded a flamboyance that was hard to ignore. He was arrested in Virginia City for "uttering disloyal sentiments" and imprisoned for three weeks at Fort Churchill, where secessionists marched about carrying heavy bags of sand as punishment. The army released him after he posted a large five thousand–dollar bond, signed the oath of allegiance, and promised to desist from statements offensive to loyal Americans. He, too, participated in organizing the Democrats, but despite his acknowledged brilliance the stigma of his imprisonment prevented his rise in postwar politics.[15]

How much truth can be sifted from the legends of secessionist plots in early Nevada? One originated with tales told by William Stewart in his dotage, when his exploits mushroomed into whoppers. Was Judge Flenniken's appointment really a pro-Southern maneuver by President Buchanan, and did Stewart force the judge to resign at gunpoint? Modern historians regard Stewart's guns with dubious eyes. Yet Flenniken did resign. Did Terry actually carry a commission from Jefferson Davis to be governor of the Confederate state of Nevada? And did he, in truth, erect two forts at the mines and bring in armed men in the belief that whoever held the mines would win the war? Terry's biographer disbelieves the Confederate commission but finds the attempt to hold mining claims by force of arms plausible as a not uncommon practice. Beneath the exaggerations there may have been a bedrock of truth.[16]

No more would the rebels erupt in pandemonium in the streets, but they were still present and still influential. In January 1864 the voters rejected the first state constitution submitted to them. Several historians conclude that the rebels influenced this outcome, though mining taxation issues loomed largest. By the time of the favorable vote on the second constitution, mining taxation and other unpopular issues had been corrected, and in the midst of an economic depression caused by a recent downturn in mining the argument that statehood would help the economy easily drowned other issues. Many Southern sympathizers probably joined Dr. McMeans and Hal Clayton in the new state Democratic Party. Though occasionally winning an office, the Democrats would remain a minority in the constellation of Nevada parties

for nearly a half century until the central Nevada mining boom at To-
nopah and Goldfield multiplied their ranks.[17]

The Nevada constitution adopted in the fall of 1864 immediately
prior to statehood and Lincoln's reelection sounded the death knell for
Confederate hopes. It contained a bold and unequivocal clause declar-
ing that every citizen owed "paramount allegiance" to the federal government, that no state had a right to secede, and if one did so "the Federal Government may, by warrant of the Constitution, employ armed
force in compelling obedience to its authority." The pugnacious language of the "paramount allegiance" clause exceeded any other state
constitution except Arkansas's, which copied it word for word in 1868.
Nevada had embraced the Union to which it owed its existence with
gratitude.[18]

The struggle was over, and in an amazingly short time. Nevadans
had been granted their territory and a scant three years later their
state. Of the elements who faced off at the beginning, the Mormons
had retreated, the Indians had been marginalized, and the old Californians ruled triumphant.[19] Whereas repeated agitation and shameless
exaggeration had kept the territorial issue alive, it took propitious national events and, above all, the excitement of the Comstock discovery
to catapult it through Congress. Not much earlier the intrepid Snowshoe Thompson, skimming over the Sierra Nevada on his skis, had
been the only link between the tiny settlements clinging to the eastern
slope and the outside world in winter. Scarcely enough time had
passed for crude trails to become roads, frame homes to replace tents,
and fledgling orchards to bear fruit. In all, just ten years had gone by
since John Reese rolled his wagons into the Carson Valley in 1851 and
set up the first permanent trading station.

Ghosts Who Walk

I N THE EARLY DAYS, Tennessee had called Nevada an emigrant trail and a mine. A century and a half later the broad outlines still fitted: emigrants still, but instead of gold rushers on their way to California sustaining Nevada traders, they are tourists sustaining casinos with their business, still drinking and gambling "in fine stile" as in the 1850s; or they are emigrants, many from California, moving in to live in America's fastest-growing city, Las Vegas, and other locales. Still the California backwash. And still mining. The Comstock has played out and been transformed into a tourist attraction, but mining continues with no end in sight at some of the world's most productive gold mines on the Carlin Trend in northeastern Nevada.[1]

Some hard times lay ahead, including a period of depression and depopulation toward the end of the nineteenth century when the Comstock mines sank into borrasca. But fortunately, there have been no events so catastrophic as those predicted by Orson Hyde when he laid a curse upon the Carson and Washoe Valleys. Infuriated because he received no payment beyond an ox team, an old worn-out wagon and harness, and a span of "small, indifferent mules" for his sawmill worth twenty thousand dollars, the so-called olive branch of Israel thundered:

> You shall be visited by the Lord of Hosts with thunder and with earthquakes and with floods, with pestilence and with famine until your

names are not known amongst men, for you have rejected the authority of God, trampled upon his laws and his ordinances, and given yourselves up to serve the god of this world; to rioting in debauchery, in abominations, drunkenness and corruption. You have chuckled and gloried in taking the property of the Mormons, and withholding from them the benefits thereof.

Hyde failed to collect and had to content himself with the oxen, the worn-out wagon, and the small, indifferent mules.[2]

Undoubtedly, the apostle's spirit sought more congenial surroundings than Nevada, where the materialistic, freewheeling, individualistic ways of the boomers prevailed and the religious community he had tried to create seemed a short and bizarre aberration. Lucky Bill Thorington swung from the gallows, but the gambler's values he represented became Nevada's. Strangely, Lucky Bill's ghost lingered in a more literal sense. Like Butch Cassidy and the Sundance Kid, like Elvis Presley, Bill lived on in the eyes of those who liked and admired him. In an implausible story that went the rounds, a physician of rare skill with an electric battery and chemical potions revived Lucky Bill's corpse, and he was seen more than twenty years later running a gambling hall in Colorado. When several Carson Valley men then dug up the coffin believed to be his, they found only rocks inside, which confirmed their belief that somehow, somewhere, Lucky Bill still lived.[3] No one believed they had seen William Ormsby tending bar in Colorado. Although he enjoyed no storied afterlife, his type would be seen again more than once—the carpetbagger aspiring politician who plans to use a thinly populated state as a springboard to high office.

Whistled up by a succession of authors in need of a spectacular villain, Sam Brown's ghost swaggered on for more than a century. These writers omitted Brown's positive qualities, steadily inflated the body count of his victims, and added embellishments to the "brutal monster, with every instinct brutish" until the farther in time one proceeds, the more a stereotype replaces the real man. The process of exaggeration culminated in 1976 in an exercise in falsity titled *Leather 'n Lead*. "In the year 1860 alone, Sam knifed sixteen men before taking their money." Brown has morphed into a gang leader, stage robber, cattle rustler, and Indian slayer. "Brown and his men sacked Piute villages, scalped the tribesmen, and raped the squaws." Brown had wanted to be known as a famous "big chief," but he might have had trouble recognizing the literary monster he had become.[4]

What ghost walks longer than a lawsuit? After his contract ended in 1860, the pioneer mail contractor George Chorpenning spent the rest of his life seeking compensation for the losses he had suffered and took his case all the way to the Supreme Court. Though none could doubt the hardships Chorpenning had undergone, including the loss of his partner to Indian attack, the scale of the payment he sought raised questions. A congressional vote in 1871 stripped him of the $443,000 granted to him by the postmaster general, and Chorpenning died poverty stricken in New York in 1894. His claims against the government did not die with him, however. In 2001, 150 years after Chorpenning began his mail runs, his descendants announced that they would press Congress to reopen the "Jackass Mail" case, as it had become known. "He was cheated by the government," a great-grandson declared. "I would like justice."[5]

No ghost walks with firmer stride than Sarah Winnemucca, now acknowledged as one of the most important pre-twentieth-century Indian women along with Pocahontas and Sacajawea. Long after her death her extraordinary courage and her many accomplishments received well-deserved recognition. In 2001 a drive by the Nevada Women's History Project led by Carrie Townley Porter and others resulted in a bill introduced in the Nevada legislature by assemblywoman Marcia DeBraga to make Sarah Winnemucca the second statue representing Nevada in U.S. Capitol Statuary Hall in Washington, D.C. The legislature enacted the measure without a dissenting vote. So Sarah returns to Washington, D.C., no longer to plead the Paiute cause to presidents and congressmen as she did in life, but this

Sculpted by artist Benjamin Victor, Sarah Winnemucca's statue representing Nevada was unveiled in 2005 at U.S. Capitol Statuary Hall, Washington, D.C. She holds a shell flower, the source of her Paiute name (Thocmetony), in one hand and her book, *Life among the Piutes,* in the other. Courtesy Ronald M. James.

time to stay, forever clasping her book in one hand and the shell flower that was the origin of her Paiute name (Thocmetony) in the other. Her statue was unveiled in the spring of 2005.[6]

The ghosts of the discoverers of the Comstock stayed sealed in their graves. They had sold out too soon for too little and spent too freely in the usual way of prospectors. Old Virginny Finney, who had been living on the charity of friends, was first to die, thrown from his horse when drunk in 1861. The bombastic Henry Comstock, who had horned in on others' claims and sold his interests for a reputed twelve thousand dollars, committed suicide in Montana in 1870. Peter O'Riley realized more from the sale of his portion of the Ophir Mine, but invested unwisely, spent the rest of his life gophering in barren granite with guidance from the spirits, and died in an insane asylum. Patrick McLaughlin sold his part of the Ophir for next to nothing, became an impoverished camp cook in California, and died a pauper. To its discoverers, the great bonanza appears to have been more potent a curse than the dark fulminations of Orson Hyde against the valley folk. But the discovery that brought them suicide, madness, poverty, and early death meant everything to the creation of Nevada.[7]

In Gold Canyon today, as you walk north from Dayton to Silver City, you can see the course of the canyon all the way by the string of misty green trees, just coming into leaf, cottonwoods, willows, and more along the creek bed. The creek is nearly all dry this spring, even after a wet winter. In only one spot does water pool in a little pond with water plants, possibly spring fed. As you walk, the canyon widens and narrows from time to time. In some places the sides are rocky and steep, so compressed that there is only space for the creek. At other less cliff-like places, the canyon walls back away into gentler hills, where the earth has a faintly rusty tinge, dotted with piñon and brilliant splashes of red Indian paintbrush and orange penstemon. The game the early prospectors hunted is nowhere in evidence, and it stretches the imagination to remember that they shot rabbits, deer, and even mountain

Gold Canyon, 2003. Author's collection.

sheep to largely live off the land. These days one can traverse the entire canyon without seeing so much as a jackrabbit.

Men have dumped their trash in several places, abandoned cars and rusted bits of mining machinery amid the usual cans and broken bottles. But nothing from the 1850s can readily be identified, not the Groshes' cabin, not even the miners' rendezvous at Johntown. Although one researcher has found a couple of foundations that might have been Johntown, no one is certain. A new mine has recently opened east of Gold Hill, but mining inside the canyon has long since ceased, except for a single prospector in a cloud of dust with a vigor-ously vibrating riffle box powered by a gasoline engine. With great pa-tience and many hours of labor, he has extracted two vials of gleaming gold flecks. He acknowledges that he continues to placer mainly be-cause he enjoys it, which the prospectors of earlier days would have understood.

In this neglected place, we stand upon historic ground, because it was in this canyon so many years ago, along this creek of rounded, water-smoothed, gray stones, lined with trees greening with spring, the gateway to the great Comstock Lode, that Nevada really began.

NOTES

Abbreviations

MD *Mountain Democrat*

TE *Territorial Enterprise*

1 · THE FIRST SETTLERS ARRIVE, 1851

1. Will Bagley, ed., *Frontiersman: Abner Blackburn's Narrative*, ix, 1–2, 21, 57, 113.

2. Bagley, *Frontiersman*, 21, 25, 57, 103; Bil Gilbert, *Westering Man: The Life of Joseph Walker*, 130–31, 146–47; Rockwell D. Hunt, *John Bidwell: Prince of California Pioneers*, 68–69; George R. Stewart, *The California Trail*, 7–27, 56–82; Mary Lee Spence and Donald Jackson, eds., *The Expeditions of John Charles Fremont*, 1:601.

3. Bagley, *Frontiersman*, 112, 115, 117–18.

4. Ibid., 101, 140. The other principal candidate for first discovery is William Prows, who claimed to have found gold in the canyon when returning from California with the Mormon Battalion in 1848. Although some have accepted his story, historian Will Bagley offers persuasive evidence invalidating it (*Frontiersman*, 133–36). An emigrant reminiscence of an 1850 journey mentions but does not date an earlier Prows discovery (Kenneth N. Owens, *History*, 162–63). Hampton S. Beatie, who traveled with Blackburn, also credits him with first discovery (*Nevada Historical Society Papers, 1913–1916*, 169–70).

5. Bagley, *Frontiersman*, 101, 140, 158–59, 171; *Nevada Historical Society Papers*, 168.

6. Bagley, *Frontiersman*, 172.

7. *Nevada Historical Society Papers*, 169; Owens, *History*, 224–25.

8. Dale L. Morgan, *The Humboldt: Highroad of the West*, 200; Bagley, *Frontiersman*, 172; *Nevada Historical Society Papers*, 169.

9. Bagley, *Frontiersman*, 172–73, 178, 183–87, 195, 201–2, 211–12, 216–17.

10. *Nevada Historical Society Papers*, 187; Bagley, *Frontiersman*, 166–67; Lynn E. Williamson, "From Our Library Collection." Historian Ronald M. James suggests that the story of Finney's death as related by Comstock journalist Dan De Quille (William Wright) (see *The Big Bonanza*, 52–53) is folklore, but it is plausible (*The Roar and the Silence: A History of Virginia City and the Comstock Lode*, 6–7, 13–14). We know from the matter-of-fact Reese that Finney drank heavily, as did many in the mining crowd, and another early source cited by James (Henry DeGroot, *The Comstock Papers*) connects Finney's death with alcohol. On May 27, 2001, a monument was dedicated to Finney in the Dayton cemetery.

11. Morgan, *Humboldt*, 201; Bagley, *Frontiersman*, 159n30, 163. The report of families at the station is somewhat puzzling, since Beatie related that the Mormons in his party left their families in Salt Lake City; this may have meant that the non-Mormons brought theirs. On the other hand, the emigrant reporting families may have mistaken members of another emigrant party for residents. See Bagley, *Frontiersman*, 163; and *Nevada Historical Society Papers*, 170–71, 188.

12. *Nevada Historical Society Papers*, 186–88; Stewart, *The California Trail*, 299–301; R. M. James, *Roar and Silence*, 5; Martin Griffith, "What's Nevada's Oldest Town?" 13; J. R. "Poker" Brown, "Testimony," 159, 165–66. For a careful analysis of early settlement, see Stanley W. Paher, "From Emigrant Trading Posts to Nevada Towns: Genoa and Dayton—but Which Was First?"

13. *Nevada Historical Society Papers*, 187–88.

14. Ibid., 190; Morgan, *Humboldt*, 213–14.

15. Morgan, *Humboldt*, 213–17.

16. Elmer Rusco, unpublished manuscript, 1–8. For further information on Nevada blacks, see Rusco, *"Good Time Coming?" Black Nevadans in the Nineteenth Century*.

17. Myron Angel, *History of Nevada*, 49.

18. Ibid., 49; Owens, *History*, 106; Michael J. Makley, *The Hanging of Lucky Bill*, 21.

19. Bret Harte, *Tales of the Gold Rush*, 54–55; Chris W. Bayer, *Profit, Plots and Lynching*, 31. On Harte's creation of the popular gold rush image through

characters such as Jack Hamlin, see Michael Kowalewski, "Romancing the Gold Rush: The Literature of the California Frontier," 219–20.

20. Angel, *History of Nevada*, 50; Harte, *Tales of the Gold Rush*, 56.

21. Bayer, *Profit, Plots and Lynching*, 30–31.

22. Ibid., 21–22.

23. Edna B. Patterson, Louise A. Ulph, and Victor Goodwin, *Nevada's Northeast Frontier*, 501.

24. *Nevada Historical Society Papers*, 176; Angel, *History of Nevada*, 528; R. M. James, *Roar and Silence*, 5.

25. The records of these meetings are printed in Angel, *History of Nevada*, 31–32. Evidently, there were two petitions. Kent D. Richards states that the one composed by a committee and unanimously approved by the settlers' meeting was never sent; however, the one composed by opponents of the Mormons independently of these meetings was submitted ("Washoe Territory: Rudimentary Government in Nevada," 215–17).

26. Angel, *History of Nevada*, 32.

27. Bagley, *Frontiersman*, 173–74.

---

2 · INDIANS, EMIGRANTS, AND GRAND IDEAS

1. Inter-Tribal Council of Nevada, *Wa She Shu: A Washo Tribal History*, 3; A. L. Kroeber, *Handbook of the Indians of California*, 570; John A. Price, "Washo Prehistory: A Review of Research," 79; U.S. Department of the Interior, *Report, 1868–1869*, 818.

2. James Downs, *The Two Worlds of the Washo: An Indian Tribe of California and Nevada*, unpaginated map; Inter-Tribal Council of Nevada, *Wa She Shu*, 51.

3. Inter-Tribal Council of Nevada, *Wa She Shu*, 5–13, 39–40; John A. Price, "Some Aspects of the Washo Life Cycle," 106. Variations on this ceremony have been reported by others.

4. Inter-Tribal Council of Nevada, *Wa She Shu*, 46; Sarah Winnemucca Hopkins, *Life among the Piutes: Their Wrongs and Claims*, 5–9.

5. Kenneth L. Holmes, ed., *Covered Wagon Women: Diaries and Letters from the Western Trails*, 4:160, 293–94.

6. James Downs, "Differential Response to White Contact," 121; George R. Stewart, *The California Trail*, 275; Kenneth N. Owens, *History*, 150.

7. Owens, *History*, 194, 335, 418, 420; Robert W. Ellison, *First Impressions: The Trail through Carson Valley, 1848–1852*, 23–24; Robert W. Ellison, *Territorial Lawmen of Nevada*, 12; Downs, *Two Worlds*, 78.

8. Owen Jones, "Recollections," *Record Courier* (Gardnerville, NV), September 4, 1925. Jones indicates that the stock thieves were horsemen, whereas Genoa lay in Washo territory and the Washo did not acquire horses until very late and then primarily as draft animals. Possibly, a few Washo had horses by 1853, or perhaps the stock thieves were Paiute, since the Paiutes had begun making inroads in Washo territory. See also Downs, "Differential Response," 124; and Downs, *Two Worlds*, 74.

9. Hopkins, *Life among the Piutes*, 14.

10. Downs, "Differential Response," 130, 132; Downs, *Two Worlds*, 78–79; Sally Zanjani, *Sarah Winnemucca*, chaps. 2–3, pp. 65–67.

11. Grace Dangberg, *Washo Tales Translated with an Introduction*, 32–47, 50–51.

12. Owens, *History*, 75; Stewart, *The California Trail*, 292. Material in this section on the California trails is primarily drawn from Kenneth N. Owens's compilation of emigrant diaries, letters, and reminiscences of travel from 1849 to 1852 (see *History*). On Royce, see Sarah Royce, *A Frontier Lady: Recollections of the Gold Rush and Early California*, 72.

13. Stewart, *The California Trail*, 107–11, 123, 224–25; Owens, *History*, 169, 260; R. W. Ellison, *First Impressions*, 71.

14. R. W. Ellison, *First Impressions*, 91–92.

15. Stewart, *The California Trail*, 207–15, 267–68, 292, 297.

16. David Morris Potter, ed., *Trail to California: The Overland Journal of Vincent Geiger and Wakeman Bryarly*, 185.

17. Mary McDougall Gordon, ed., *Overland to California with the Pioneer Line: The Gold Rush Diary of Bernard J. Reid*, 125, 130; Potter, *Trail to California*, 193n9, 195; Owens, *History*, 304; Sessions S. Wheeler, *The Nevada Desert*, 30.

18. Owens, *History*, 117, 278.

19. R. W. Ellison, *First Impressions*, 48; Owens, *History*, 246.

20. Helen S. Carlson, *Nevada Place Names: A Geographical Dictionary*, 197; Gordon, *Overland to California*, 120.

21. R. W. Ellison, *First Impressions*, 23; Dale L. Morgan, *The Humboldt: Highroad of the West*, 200.

22. Owens, *History*, 88, 167.

23. Ibid., 195, 221, 283, 321, 340.

24. Ibid., 173, 364.

25. Holmes, *Covered Wagon Women*, 4:79–80.

26. Frederick Merk, *Manifest Destiny and Mission in American History: A Reinterpretation*, 24.

27. Earl Pomeroy, *The Pacific Slope: A History of California, Oregon, Washington, Idaho, Utah, and Nevada*, 41.

28. On old Californians, see David A. Johnson, *Founding the Far West: California, Oregon, and Nevada, 1840–1890*, 71–73, 191.

29. Dale L. Morgan, "The State of Deseret," 81–82, 87.

30. Ibid., unpaginated map, 86, 93; Leonard J. Arrington and Davis Bitton, *The Mormon Experience: A History of the Latter-Day Saints*, 162–63; Will Bagley, *Blood of the Prophets: Brigham Young and the Massacre at Mountain Meadows*, 49; John Hyde, Jun., *Mormonism: Its Leaders and Designs*, 173–74. Hyde, although an intemperate critic of the Mormons, does support his argument with direct quotations from Joseph Smith and Mormon leaders.

31. Morgan, "The State of Deseret," 128; James M. McPherson, *Battle Cry of Freedom: The Civil War Era*, 47–58; Richard White, *It's Your Misfortune and None of My Own: A New History of the American West*, 76–83.

32. Bernard DeVoto, *The Year of Decision, 1846*, 284–85; McPherson, *Battle Cry*, 58, 66–67; Morgan, "The State of Deseret," 92, 116, 126.

33. McPherson, *Battle Cry*, 74; Morgan, "The State of Deseret," 125; Leonard J. Arrington, *The Mormons in Nevada*, 10; Bagley, *Blood of the Prophets*, 43.

34. Richard V. Francaviglia, "Maps and Mining: Some Historical Examples from the Great Basin," 67. On population, see Jack E. Eblen, *The First and Second United States Empires: Governors and Territorial Government, 1784–1912*, 229–30; and Polly Aird, "Escape from Zion: The United States Army Escort of Mormon Apostates, 1859," 208, 233n45. Orson Hyde estimated about four hundred inhabitants in 1855 on the eastern slope, but he may not have included the miners (Myrtle S. Hyde, *Orson Hyde: The Olive Branch of Israel*, 338).

35. Eblen, *First and Second Empires*, 227–29; Johnson, *Founding the Far West*, 73; Arrington and Bitton, *Mormon Experience*, 163.

36. John M. Townley, "Stalking Horse for the Pony Express: The Chorpenning Mail Contracts between California and Utah, 1851–1860," 229–37. On the transportation revolution, see McPherson, *Battle Cry*, 11–13.

37. Myron Angel, *History of Nevada*, 103–4.

3 · THE CURSED BLACK STUFF

1. Austin E. Hutcheson, "Before the Comstock: Memoirs of William Hickman Dolman," 245; Dan De Quille, *The Big Bonanza*, 19. Figures on the Comstock's yield from 1859 to 1919 are from Grant H. Smith, *The History of the Comstock Lode*, 292–93, 297.

2. Eliot Lord, *Comstock Mining and Miners*, 13, 24n1; Kenneth N. Owens, *History*, 215.

3. Hosea Ballou Grosh to father, November 22, 1856, Ethan Allen and Hosea Ballou Grosh Papers, 1849–1857. The letter alludes to the Mexican company Old Frank accompanied as silver miners. If this was fact and not assumption, Old Frank's companions would have recognized silver. Also see Henry T. P. Comstock, *Chronology of the Comstock Lode*, n.p.; and Charles H. Shinn, *The Story of the Mine*, 29. Shinn, drawing on the Hoover manuscript, dates Antonio's trip in July 1853, but since the Grosh brothers were already planning to go to Gold Canyon based on his information in March 1853, it appears likely that Antonio may have been there in 1852.

4. Leonetto Cipriani, *California and Overland Diaries*, 1, 10–14, 72–73.

5. Ibid., 127.

6. Ibid., 127–28.

7. Shinn, *Story of the Mine*, 27–29; Charles T. Wegman, telephone interview with author, March 6, 2002.

8. Father to E. A. Grosh, October 25, 1857; H. B. Grosh to father, March 31, 1850; E. A. Grosh to father, September 29, 1849, April 30, May 30, 1850, January 5, 1851, Grosh Papers. On the forty-niners, see Malcolm J. Rohrbough, *Days of Gold: The California Gold Rush and the American Nation*, 32–33.

9. H. B. Grosh to father, August 17, 1851, with postscript (probably E. A. Grosh), September 1851; and March 6, 1853, Grosh Papers.

10. E. A. Grosh to father, October 31, 1849, April 30, 1850, January 5, 12, 1851, and n.d., ibid.; Wegman interview.

11. E. A. Grosh and H. B. Grosh to father, March 26, May 22, July 13, 1853, Grosh Papers.

12. Ibid., November 22, 1856, October 5, 1853; H. B. Grosh to father, December 3, 1853; Lord, *Comstock Mining and Miners*, 16, 24; J. R. Brown, "Testimony," 162; Captain Parker, "Testimony," 175.

13. E. A. Grosh and H. B. Grosh to father, October 5, 1853, Grosh Papers;

Lord, *Comstock Mining and Miners,* 16; Shinn, *Story of the Mine,* 20; H. B. Grosh to father, December 3, 1853, Grosh Papers.

14. E. A. Grosh to father, November 8, 1854, July 29, 1855, Grosh Papers.

15. Ibid., July 29, 1855.

---

4 · THE MORMONS TAKE CHARGE, 1855

1. George R. Stewart, *The California Trail,* 310–12; Kenneth N. Owens, *History,* 446.

2. Owens, *History,* 439; Myron Angel, *History of Nevada,* 35, 37; Eliot Lord, *Comstock Mining and Miners,* 24; Robert W. Ellison, *Territorial Lawmen of Nevada,* 80; *MD,* August 12, 1854; De Quille, *The Big Bonanza,* 10–11; Stanley W. Paher, "From Emigrant Trading Posts to Nevada Towns: Genoa and Dayton—but Which Was First?" 145–47. The first mill was the Cary mill, the second a saw- and gristmill constructed for Reese. Both were built by Thomas Knott.

3. Michael J. Makley, *The Hanging of Lucky Bill,* 25–26.

4. Sam P. Davis, "Ormsby County," 2:975.

5. Sally Zanjani, "Sam Brown: The Evolution of a Frontier Villain," 6; *Sacramento Union,* April 25, May 5, 1854; *San Francisco Chronicle,* May 1, 1892.

6. Zanjani, "Sam Brown," 6; Angel, *History of Nevada,* 343.

7. N. A. Hummel, *General History and Resources of Washoe County, Nevada,* 5; Angel, *History of Nevada,* 36.

8. John M. Townley, *Tough Little Town on the Truckee, 1868–1900,* 40–41; R. W. Ellison, *Territorial Lawmen of Nevada,* 122n24. On the location of H. H. Jameson's station, see Stanley W. Paher, ed., *Emigrant Shadows,* 190.

9. James T. Butler, *Isaac Roop: Pioneer and Political Leader of Northeastern California,* 2–3, 19.

10. Ibid., 19, 20, 26. The "cheaf" who initially visited Roop was not named, but since Honey Lake Valley lay within Winnemucca's range, he was probably the one. On the relationship between Winnemucca and the Roops, see Sally Zanjani, *Sarah Winnemucca,* 94, 232.

11. John Koontz, *Political History of Nevada, 1965,* 37–40.

12. Russell R. Elliott, *History of Nevada,* 53; Koontz, *Political History of Nevada,* 40–45.

13. Angel, *History of Nevada,* 37; Leonard J. Arrington, *Great Basin King-*

dom, 88; Stanley W. Paher, *Las Vegas: As It Began—As It Grew*, 19–32. Though most left in March 1857, a few Mormon missionaries remained at Las Vegas until September 1858.

14. Leonard J. Arrington, *Brigham Young: American Moses*, 174.

15. Ibid., 66, 71, 194; Kate B. Carter, *The Mormons in Nevada*, 438; Norman F. Furniss, *The Mormon Conflict, 1850–1859*, 19; Myrtle S. Hyde, *Orson Hyde: The Olive Branch of Israel*, 366; John Hyde, Jun., *Mormonism: Its Leaders and Designs*, 195.

16. M. S. Hyde, *Orson Hyde*, 328–29; Elliott, *History of Nevada*, 54–55; Albert R. Page, "Orson Hyde and the Carson Valley Mission, 1855–1857," 22. The excerpts from Hyde's letters to Young presented by Page provide valuable sources on this period. On Mormon colonization practices, see Leonard J. Arrington and Davis Bitton, *The Mormon Experience: A History of the Latter-Day Saints*, 120.

17. M. S. Hyde, *Orson Hyde*, 344; Page, "Orson Hyde," 35, 49; Lord, *Comstock Mining and Miners*, 17.

18. M. S. Hyde, *Orson Hyde*, 337–44, 346–49; Page, "Orson Hyde," 44, 54n7. On the 1852 survey, see Juanita Brooks, "The Mormons in Carson County, Utah Territory," 14–15. Hyde's treatment by Dr. Charles Daggett, among the first recorded medical episodes on the eastern slope, involved gradual thawing, still an appropriate approach today (Ryan Davis, "Charles Daggett: Nevada's First Doctor," 1).

19. M. S. Hyde, *Orson Hyde*, 337, 350–53, 358; Page, "Orson Hyde," 67; Hubert Howe Bancroft, *History of Nevada, 1540–1888*, 79. On "lying for the Lord," see Will Bagley, *Blood of the Prophets: Brigham Young and the Massacre at Mountain Meadows*, 41–42.

20. Page, "Orson Hyde," 65n3, 72; J. Hyde, *Mormonism*, 190–91.

21. Page, "Orson Hyde," 70–71, 77, 81.

22. Ibid., 20–21, 36, 49–50, 113n5.

23. M. S. Hyde, *Orson Hyde*, 337; Page, "Orson Hyde," 36–38, 51, 59, 90–92.

24. M. S. Hyde, *Orson Hyde*, 341; Bancroft, *History*, 76; R. W. Ellison, *Territorial Lawmen of Nevada*, 9–14, 34–36; Furniss, *Mormon Conflict*, 57.

25. Elliott, *History of Nevada*, 55; James G. Scrugham, *Nevada*, 1:124; Page, "Orson Hyde," 53; M. S. Hyde, *Orson Hyde*, 371–72, 403, 405, 420.

26. M. S. Hyde, *Orson Hyde*, 356–57; H. Hamlin, ed., *Knott Reminiscences*, 7–8; R. W. Ellison, *Territorial Lawmen of Nevada*, 110, 113–14, 188–91. On the

subsequent decline and fall of the disreputable Drummond, see Furniss, *Mormon Conflict*, 54–55.

27. Angel, *History of Nevada*, 39; M. S. Hyde, *Orson Hyde*, 359; Page, "Orson Hyde," 87–89; R. W. Ellison, *Territorial Lawmen of Nevada*, 107, 115–16. The Mormon ticket included a few non-Mormons who were considered pro-Mormon.

28. Page, "Orson Hyde," 87–90.

29. Furniss, *Mormon Conflict*, 11–15; Arrington and Bitton, *Mormon Experience*, 59–60. On immigrants, see David Morris Potter, *The Impending Crisis, 1848-1861*, 241–43.

30. Arrington, *Great Basin Kingdom*, 62–63; J. Hyde, *Mormonism*, 307; Furniss, *Mormon Conflict*, 80.

31. Page, "Orson Hyde," 54–55; M. S. Hyde, *Orson Hyde*, 342.

---

5 · JAMES CRANE EXPLAINS IT ALL, 1857

1. Chris W. Bayer, *Profit, Plots and Lynching*, 46–47, 100; Robert W. Ellison, *Territorial Lawmen of Nevada*, 138–39n9.

2. Guy L. Rocha, "How Nevada Became 'Nevada,'" 71; Bayer, *Profit, Plots and Lynching*, 47.

3. Sally Zanjani, *Sarah Winnemucca*, 45–51.

4. Kent D. Richards, "Washoe Territory: Rudimentary Government in Nevada," 220–21; Louis J. Rasmussen, *San Francisco Ship Passenger Lists*, 73–74; James G. Scrugham, *Nevada*, 1:127–29; Lester J. Cappon, *Virginia Newspapers, 1821-1935*, 185. Several copies of the *Southerner* have been preserved in the Rare Books and Special Collections Library at Duke University, Durham, NC.

5. Henry DeGroot, *The Comstock Papers*, 17–18; Bayer, *Profit, Plots and Lynching*, 61; James Crane, letter dated February 3, 1857, in *Alta California*, February 4, 1857.

6. Bayer, *Profit, Plots and Lynching*, 80–82, 87–88.

7. R. W. Ellison, *Territorial Lawmen of Nevada*, 319. On the Pacific Republic, see also Joseph Ellison, "Designs for a Pacific Republic"; Dorothy Hull, "The Movement in Oregon for the Establishment of a Pacific Coast Republic," 177–200; and Elijah R. Kennedy, *The Contest for California in 1861*, 24–31.

8. James M. Crane, *The Past, the Present and the Future of the Pacific*, 9, 12, 26–30, 38, 43–44, 56.

9. Ibid., 76–77, 79.

10. Myron Angel, *History of Nevada*, 42–43; Bayer, *Profit, Plots and Lynching*, 60, 62.

11. Angel, *History of Nevada*, 43–45.

12. Ibid., 44–45. Estimates on Indian populations were questionable and shifting, as disease, warfare, and starvation decreased the numbers. One of the earliest estimates, in an 1868 Indian agent's report, listed 8,200 in the Nevada superintendency (including 1,500 Bannocks, evidently in error, and omitting Southern Paiutes, at least as a separate group) (U.S. Department of the Interior, *Report, 1868–1869*, 818).

13. *MD*, October 24, 1857; Bayer, *Profit, Plots and Lynching*, 79.

14. David Thompson, *The Tennessee Letters: From Carson Valley, 1857–1860*, 80; Russell R. Elliott, *History of Nevada*, 58; Bayer, *Profit, Plots and Lynching*, 63–67. On frontier factions, see Howard R. Lamar, *Dakota Territory, 1861–1889: A Study of Frontier Politics*, 16. On the high reputation of the California vigilance committees among contemporaries, see George R. Stewart, *Committee of Vigilance*, 316.

15. Bayer, *Profit, Plots and Lynching*, 65. The California newspaper sources cited on this episode are somewhat conflicting.

16. Norman F. Furniss, *The Mormon Conflict, 1850–1859*, 58–59, 67, 76–77, 92–94; Leonard J. Arrington and Davis Bitton, *The Mormon Experience: A History of the Latter-Day Saints*, 164–65.

17. Furniss, *Mormon Conflict*, 66–67, 77–80; Richard White, *It's Your Misfortune and None of My Own: A New History of the American West*, 168; Leonard J. Arrington, *Brigham Young: American Moses*, 251–52.

18. Will Bagley, *Blood of the Prophets: Brigham Young and the Massacre at Mountain Meadows*, 62, 73–75; Furniss, *Mormon Conflict*, 63, 67; White, *It's Your Misfortune*, 168.

19. Furniss, *Mormon Conflict*, 68–69.

6 · The Mormons Depart, the Groshes Return, 1857

1. Kate B. Carter, *The Mormons in Nevada*, 442–43.

2. Ibid., 445–46; Will Bagley, *Blood of the Prophets: Brigham Young and the Massacre at Mountain Meadows*, 193. Figures vary on how much money was collected: according to Conover, $12,160, a high sum for that time and place (446); Madison D. Hambleton, in the account the Mormon Church considered

official, placed it at $800 (Juanita Brooks, "The Mormons in Carson County, Utah Territory," 22); Juanita Brooks pegs it at $1,260 (perhaps the sum credited to Conover was a mistaken rendering of this one) (*The Mountain Meadows Massacre*, 17).

3. Carter, *The Mormons in Nevada*, 447–48.

4. Ibid., 449, 455, 457; Chester W. Cheel, "Historic Development of Western Utah between 118 and 120 Degrees West Longitude, 1827–1861," 28; Brooks, "Mormons in Carson County," 22. This figure is taken from the official church account of the exodus, but others vary: 985 people and 148 wagons in a newspaper account written in Genoa (Brooks, "Mormons in Carson County," 22); 968 people in a *New York Tribune* report in Effie Mona Mack, *Nevada*, 169–70.

5. Brooks, *The Mountain Meadows Massacre*, 52–53, 104, 163, 216. The plaque placed at the site in 1932 puts the number of the slain at "about 140 emigrants." See also Emily Eakin, "Reopening a Mormon Murder Mystery."

6. Eakin, "Murder Mystery"; Bagley, *Blood of the Prophets*, 382.

7. Leonard J. Arrington, *Brigham Young: American Moses*, 256–60; Eakin, "Murder Mystery."

8. Norman F. Furniss, *The Mormon Conflict, 1850–1859*, 108, 126; Brooks, *The Mountain Meadows Massacre*, 16, 99n6, 112.

9. Brooks, *The Mountain Meadows Massacre*, 86–97, 103, 105–7, 113, 118–19, 128–30, 136n4; Eakin, "Murder Mystery."

10. Kenneth L. Holmes, ed., *Covered Wagon Women: Diaries and Letters from the Western Trails*, 7:244–53; Eakin, "Murder Mystery" (Twain quote). On potential trade, see the *MD*, December 26, 1857.

11. Rodman W. Paul, *California Gold: The Beginning of Mining in the Far West*, 171–78; Eliot Lord, *Comstock Mining and Miners*, 21–24. On the Fraser River rush, see Robert E. Ficken, "The Fraser River Humbug: Americans and Gold in the British Pacific Northwest." This population estimate is primarily based on Brooks, "Mormons in Carson County," 19–20, drawn from an *Alta California* estimate of July 9, 1857; it does not include Indians, Chinese, or any inhabitants east of the eastern slope settlers or in Honey Lake. Twenty-five Truckee Meadows settlers were added as estimated in John M. Townley, *Tough Little Town on the Truckee, 1868–1900*, 42. Following Lord, *Comstock Mining and Miners*, the number of Gold Canyon miners was reduced to twenty-five from the higher figure in Brooks, with the caveat that this sector of the population underwent large fluctuations.

12. E. A. Grosh to father, July 29, 1855, September 18, 1856; E. A. Grosh and

H. B. Grosh to father, March 29, 31, August 16, November 3, 1856, Ethan Allen and Hosea Ballou Grosh Papers, 1849–1857. For a scathing analysis of John Charles Frémont's career, see Bernard DeVoto, *The Year of Decision, 1846,* 471–81.

13. E. A. Grosh and H. B. Grosh to father, August 16, 1856, Grosh Papers.

14. Ibid., November 22, 1856; E. A. to father, January 24, 1857.

15. E. A. Grosh and H. B. Grosh to father, November 22, 1856, June 8, August 16, 1857; "Article of Association of the Utah Enterprize Mining Company," May 20, 1857, Grosh Papers.

16. E. A. Grosh and H. B. Grosh to father, November 22, 1856; E. A. Grosh to father, January 24, 1857, Grosh Papers.

17. E. A. Grosh and H. B. Grosh to father, August 23, 1857, ibid.; Chris W. Bayer, *Profit, Plots and Lynching,* 64.

18. E. A. Grosh to father, 7 September 1857, Grosh Papers.

19. Ibid.

20. Ibid., September 11, 1857; Bucke to A. B. Grosh, February 10, 1858, ibid.

21. Bucke to A. B. Grosh, February 10, 1858, ibid.

22. Ibid.; E. A. Grosh to "Gov. and Friend" (Francis J. Hoover), December 12, 1857; E. A. Grosh to father, September 7, 1857, ibid.

23. Angel, *History of Nevada,* 51–52; Charles H. Shinn, *The Story of the Mine,* 29, 33–34. The last letter Allen wrote (see note 22) had been directed to Hoover.

24. Austin E. Hutcheson, "Before the Comstock: Memoirs of William Hickman Dolman," 216, 235.

25. Ibid., 220, 233–35; Grant H. Smith, *The History of the Comstock Lode,* 4.

26. Benjamin R. Nickerson, *A Statement of the Grounds of the Claim of the Grosch Consolidated Gold and Silver Mining Company, to the Comstock Mine in Nevada Territory: Together with Their Reply to the Attacks of the Press.* The lawsuit was reported in various newspapers: for example, the *Gold Hill News,* October 20, 1863, and the *Virginia Evening Bulletin,* August 5, 11, 1863; the sale by the Grosh heirs to the speculators was recounted in the *Bulletin.*

27. Lord, *Comstock Mining and Miners,* 133; G. H. Smith, *History of the Comstock Lode,* 4, 70.

7 · DEVILS REIGN, 1858

1. Although a résumé with the collection places the Browns' arrival in 1856, the date of the first letter from the eastern slope (September 5, 1857) and the purchase of Mormon land indicate 1857. Although the financial arrangements for the first drive are unstated, they probably involved a loan and a paternal investment in livestock. Peleg Brown to father, November 11, 1852; to Lydia, April 21, 1857; to parents, Jan 11, June, 21, 1857, Peleg Brown Papers. Barbara Harmon, telephone interview, April 4, 2003.

2. P. Brown to sister, September 11, 1857; to parents, February 15, 1858, P. Brown Papers. See also Benjamin Damonte Papers.

3. P. Brown to sister, September 11, 26 (an appended note to September 11), 1857, January 3, 1858; to parents, July 28, 1858; to sister and brother, October 10, 1857, P. Brown Papers.

4. P. Brown to Lydia, April 16, 1858; to sister, January 3, 1858, January 9, 1859 (note appended to December 30, 1858); to parents, September 23, 1857, February 15, 16, May, 12, 1858; to sister and brother, October 10, 1857, ibid.

5. P. Brown to parents, February 15, April 16, 1858, ibid.

6. Ibid., February 15, 1858; to brother, February 15, 1858.

7. P. Brown to brother, October 12, 1857; to father, October 8?, 1857; to parents, February 15, April 16, 1858, ibid.

8. P. Brown to sister, January 3, 1858; to Pardon, February 16, 1858; to Lydia, April 16, 1858, ibid.; Norman F. Furniss, *The Mormon Conflict, 1850–1859*, 134–35; Juanita Brooks, *The Mountain Meadows Massacre*, 112–13; Leonard J. Arrington and Davis Bitton, *The Mormon Experience: A History of the Latter-Day Saints*, 168–69.

9. Kent D. Richards, "Washoe Territory: Rudimentary Government in Nevada," 222–23; Myron Angel, *History of Nevada*, 46; Guy L. Rocha, "How Nevada Became 'Nevada,'" 71.

10. Angel, *History of Nevada*, 46; Rocha, "How Nevada Became 'Nevada,'" 71; Richards, "Washoe Territory," 223; Howard R. Lamar, *Dakota Territory, 1861–1889: A Study of Frontier Politics*, 55; P. Brown to parents, July 28, 1858, P. Brown Papers. On the Kansas-Nebraska issue, see David Morris Potter, *The Impending Crisis, 1848–1861*, 328–30.

11. J. Brown to father, August 2, 1858; P. Brown to Lydia, April 28, 30 (note appended), 1858; to parents, February 15, July 28, 1858; to brother, October

22, 1858; to sister, January 27, 1859, P. Brown Papers. See also Damonte Papers.

12. Myra S. Ratay, *Pioneers of the Ponderosa*, 59–60. On vigilantism, see also William Burrows, *Vigilante!* 6–14; and Richard Maxwell Brown, *No Duty to Retreat: Violence and Values in American History and Society*, 131.

13. Asa M. Fairfield, *A Pioneer History of Lassen County*, 124–27.

14. H. Hamlin, ed., *Knott Reminiscences*, 11; Fairfield, *Pioneer History*, 124–27.

15. Fairfield, *Pioneer History*, 132–36.

16. Michael J. Makley, *The Hanging of Lucky Bill*, 53–54, 59; Fairfield, *Pioneer History*, 136–37, 140.

17. Robert W. Ellison, *Territorial Lawmen of Nevada*, 171n45; Fairfield, *Pioneer History*, 137.

18. Angel, *History of Nevada*, 50–51; *Nevada Historical Society Papers, 1913–1916*, 191; Makley, *Hanging of Lucky Bill*, 101–2, 106–7; Chris W. Bayer, *Profit, Plots and Lynching*, 102; Fairfield, *Pioneer History*, 141–42.

19. Beatrice F. Jones, "Hanging of Lucky Bill," 12; Bayer, *Profit, Plots and Lynching*, 103; Arnold R. Trimmer, "Reminiscences of the Number One Ranch in Carson Valley, Nevada," 36; Makley, *Hanging of Lucky Bill*, 107.

20. *Nevada Historical Society Papers*, 191–92; Trimmer, "Reminiscences," 181–82; Fairfield, *Pioneer History*, 128–29, 140–43; Makley, *Hanging of Lucky Bill*, 57, 90.

21. Makley, *Hanging of Lucky Bill*, 108–10.

22. R. W. Ellison, *Territorial Lawmen of Nevada*, 163, 168, 170nn38–39; Fairfield, *Pioneer History*, 143; Makley, *Hanging of Lucky Bill*, 111.

23. Lillis Hunter, telephone interview with author, August 8, 2001, May 6, 2003; Leonard Olds, telephone interview with author, July 31, 2003; Makley, *Hanging of Lucky Bill*, 111–12. On Round Valley, see Willie A. Chalfant, *The Story of Inyo*, 165, 208, 213–14, 226, 228.

24. *MD*, June 28, 1858; Makley, *Hanging of Lucky Bill*, 105, 107.

25. Helmut Schoeck, *Envy: A Theory of Social Behavior*, 8. On Elliott's gambling, see R. W. Ellison, *Territorial Lawmen of Nevada*, 158.

26. R. W. Ellison, *Territorial Lawmen of Nevada*, 179; Bayer, *Profit, Plots and Lynching*, 118; David Thompson, *The Tennessee Letters: From Carson Valley, 1857–1860*, 56.

27. Angel, *History of Nevada*, 49; R. W. Ellison, *Territorial Lawmen of Nevada*, 177–80. In Angel's account, four of six precincts were discarded.

28. R. W. Ellison, *Territorial Lawmen of Nevada*, 177–78, 183, 186; Don West, "Troubled Days in Carson Valley," 55.

29. Angel, *History of Nevada*, 104, 106; Bayer, *Profit, Plots and Lynching*, 103; John M. Townley, "Stalking Horse for the Pony Express: The Chorpenning Mail Contracts between California and Utah, 1851–1860," 246; Richard E. Lingenfelter and Karen R. Gash, *The Newspapers of Nevada: A History and Bibliography, 1854–1979*, 87–91.

30. Thompson, *Tennessee Letters*, 19; Bayer, *Profit, Plots and Lynching*, 113.

8 · BONANZA, 1859

1. David Thompson, *The Tennessee Letters: From Carson Valley, 1857–1860*, 35, 43; Peleg Brown to Lydia, March 7, 1859; to parents, March 27, 1859, Peleg Brown Papers.

2. Thompson, *Tennessee Letters*, 35–37, 42, 46, 52.

3. Ibid., 22, 45, 49–50; Sally Zanjani, *Sarah Winnemucca*, 52–53; P. Brown to father, April 15, 1859; to Lydia, March 7, 1859, P. Brown Papers.

4. Thompson, *Tennessee Letters*, 24, 38, 41–42, 48, 56–58; H. Hamlin, ed., *Knott Reminiscences*, 8; Grant H. Smith, *The History of the Comstock Lode*, 2–6. See also Benjamin Damonte Papers.

5. G. H. Smith, *History of the Comstock Lode*, 2–6; Ronald M. James, *The Roar and the Silence: A History of Virginia City and the Comstock Lode*, 6–11.

6. G. H. Smith, *History of the Comstock Lode*, 6; Dan De Quille, *The Big Bonanza*, 24–25.

7. Hubert Howe Bancroft, *History of Nevada, 1540–1888*, 98n8; De Quille, *The Big Bonanza*, 20–21; G. H. Smith, *History of the Comstock Lode*, 7. Dates of Comstock's arrival in Gold Canyon vary. Bancroft places it in 1856, and, in a letter written later from Montana, Comstock places it in 1854. Because much in this letter is patently false, and, as De Quille notes, it reveals a "wavering mind," I have considered Bancroft's date more likely.

8. Charles H. Shinn, *The Story of the Mine*, 42; R. M. James, *Roar and Silence*, 8–9. For a skeptical assessment of the sources on early Comstockers, see R. M. James, *Roar and Silence*, 14–20.

9. G. H. Smith, *History of the Comstock Lode*, 3; Austin E. Hutcheson, "A Life of Fifty Years in Nevada: The Memoirs of Penrod of the Comstock Lode, Commentary, Notes, and Transcription by Austin E. Hutcheson," 134; Austin

E. Hutcheson, "Before the Comstock: Memoirs of William Hickman Dolman," 240.

10. G. H. Smith, *History of the Comstock Lode*, 9–10; R. M. James, *Roar and Silence*, 11; De Quille, *The Big Bonanza*, 11–12, 33. In *Tough Little Town on the Truckee, 1868–1900*, John M. Townley identifies the station keeper as John F. Stone, from the station where Beckwourth Trail branches off from the main Truckee route (50–53).

11. De Quille, *The Big Bonanza*, 33.

12. P. Brown to Lydia, June 18, 1859; to brother, July 12, 1859, P. Brown Papers; N. A. Hummel, *General History and Resources of Washoe County, Nevada*, 134.

13. P. Brown to brother, November 12, 1859, P. Brown Papers.

14. P. Brown to Pardon, November 11, 1859; to brother, November 12, 1859; to parents, October 8, 1859, ibid. Beef prices on the Sacramento market in 1860 suggest that Peleg had good reason to be excited (see David Vaught, "After the Gold Rush: Replicating the Rural Midwest in the Sacramento Valley," 452).

15. Thompson, *Tennessee Letters*, 99, 103; G. H. Smith, *History of the Comstock Lode*, 15–16; Henry DeGroot, *The Comstock Papers*, 19–20; *TE*, December 17, 1859.

16. G. H. Smith, *History of the Comstock Lode*, 19; Thompson, *Tennessee Letters*, 99, 103, 106; R. M. James, *Roar and Silence*, 12.

17. De Quille, *The Big Bonanza*, 37; DeGroot, *The Comstock Papers*, 23–24.

18. *TE*, April 9, 1859. The speaker was a South Carolinian who doubted that Nevada would support slavery (see Michael W. Bowers, *The Sagebrush State: Nevada's History, Government, and Politics*, 11).

19. Thompson, *Tennessee Letters*, 58–59; *TE*, July 19, 1859.

20. *TE*, July 9, 19, 1859; Thompson, *Tennessee Letters*, 60, 68, 70, 82; Kenneth N. Owens, "Government and Politics in the Nineteenth-Century West," 150–51; Myron Angel, *History of Nevada*, 62–66, 69–72; Russell R. Elliott, *History of Nevada*, 67–68. Kent D. Richards suggests that Crane played a leading role in the drive for a constitution and a provisional government ("Washoe Territory: Rudimentary Government in Nevada," 226–27), but I have been unable to substantiate this. The *Territorial Enterprise*, which had earlier reported a large majority for Dodge (July 19), later contended that the Dodge vote was fraudulent because much of it had been cast by transients (see November 26, 1859); Dodge was an agent for the Carson Valley Agency of the

Utah Superintendency (Edward E. Hill, *The Office of Indian Affairs, 1824–1880: Historical Sketches,* 108).

21. *TE,* April 9, October 8, 1859; Thompson, *Tennessee Letters,* 72, 74, 90, 102; Richards, "Washoe Territory," 225; *Nevada Historical Society Papers, 1913–1916,* 174–75.

22. Thompson, *Tennessee Letters,* 101–2.

23. Ibid., 87, 103; Richards, "Washoe Territory," 226.

24. *TE,* November 26, 1859; Thompson, *Tennessee Letters,* 69.

25. *TE,* December 17, 1859. David A. Johnson ascribes the collapse of the provisional government to the mining rush (*Founding the Far West: California, Oregon, and Nevada, 1840–1890,* 74–75).

26. Russell R. Elliott, *Servant of Power: A Political Biography of Senator William M. Stewart,* 10–11; Henry Nash Smith, ed., *Mark Twain of the "Enterprise,"* 97.

27. Thompson, *Tennessee Letters,* 76; G. H. Smith, *History of the Comstock Lode,* 9, 14–18; Hutcheson, "Before the Comstock," 233.

---

9 · An Indian for Breakfast and a Pony to Ride, 1860

1. J. Ross Browne, *A Peep at Washoe and Washoe Revisited,* 16; Myron Angel, *History of Nevada,* 66; Grant H. Smith, *The History of the Comstock Lode,* 21; David Thompson, *The Tennessee Letters: From Carson Valley, 1857–1860,* 118.

2. Browne, *Peep at Washoe,* 24–52, 93–95.

3. Ibid., 55, 57, 64, 66, 68–69.

4. Ibid., 117–21, 124–27.

5. Ronald M. James, *The Roar and the Silence: A History of Virginia City and the Comstock Lode,* 24; G. H. Smith, *History of the Comstock Lode,* 20; Browne, *Peep at Washoe,* 126; *TE,* April 5, 1860; Thompson, *Tennessee Letters,* 128.

6. Robert M. Utley, *Frontiersmen in Blue: The United States Army and the Indian, 1848–1865,* 101, 170, 173, 180–200; Brigham D. Madsen, *The Bannock of Idaho,* 89–101; John D. McDermott, *A Guide to the Indian Wars of the West,* 16–17; James A. Sandos, "'Because He Is a Liar and a Thief': Conquering the Residents of 'Old' California, 1850–1860," 96–97; Alvin M. Josephy, *The Indian Heritage of America,* 332–33, map on 317.

7. Sarah Winnemucca Hopkins, *Life among the Piutes: Their Wrongs and*

Claims, 73–75, 51; Inter-Tribal Council of Nevada, *Numa: A Northern Paiute History,* 64–65; Sally Zanjani, *Sarah Winnemucca,* 16–17, 24–25, 40, 52, 55–56, 95, chap. 2; McDermott, *Guide to the Indian Wars,* 107.

8. Peleg Brown to father, April 4, 1859; to Lydia, March 7, 1859, Peleg Brown Papers; Thompson, *Tennessee Letters,* 124–36; *TE,* May 5, 1860; B. D. Madsen, *The Bannock of Idaho,* 104, 123; Angel, *History of Nevada,* 150–51. No definitive population figures for the Paiutes are available at this early date; in 1868 the Indian agent's count was forty-two hundred (Zanjani, *Sarah Winnemucca,* 116).

9. Thompson, *Tennessee Letters,* 84; Zanjani, *Sarah Winnemucca,* 60; Angel, *History of Nevada,* 151; Hopkins, *Life among the Piutes,* 70–71. Although another version, also recounting the rape of a Paiute female, exists, the Inter-Tribal Council of Nevada considers Winnemucca's account, probably originating with her brother Natches, a participant in the attack on Williams Station, to be accurate (*Numa,* 27–28).

10. R. M. James, *Roar and Silence,* 40; Dan De Quille, *The Big Bonanza,* 79; P. Brown to Lydia, June 17, 1860, P. Brown Papers; Thompson, *Tennessee Letters,* 135, 140; *TE,* May 19, 1860; McDermott, *Guide to the Indian Wars,* 65.

11. Angel, *History of Nevada,* 153–58. Myron Angel's account of the battle is particularly valuable because his researcher later interviewed both white and Paiute participants.

12. Ibid.

13. William C. Miller, "The Pyramid Lake Indian War of 1860," pt. 2, 105; Angel, *History of Nevada,* 158; Ferol Egan, *Sand in a Whirlwind: The Paiute Indian War of 1860,* 155; H. Hamlin, ed., *Knott Reminiscences,* 14. Ronald M. James places the death toll even higher, at seventy-six (*Roar and Silence,* 40).

14. Utley, *Frontiersmen in Blue,* 9, 62, 81; McDermott, *Guide to the Indian Wars,* 52, 104.

15. Henry DeGroot, *The Comstock Papers,* 25; Hamlin, *Knott Reminiscences,* 6; George R. Brown, ed., *Reminiscences of Senator William M. Stewart of Nevada,* 124; Miller, "Pyramid Lake Indian War," pt. 2, 104.

16. Angel, *History of Nevada,* 161–62; Miller, "Pyramid Lake Indian War," pt. 1, 47; Sam P. Davis, ed., *History of Nevada,* 1:65, 67–68. Anecdotal reports of large Paiute casualties have not been considered credible.

17. Hubert Howe Bancroft, *History of Nevada, 1540–1888,* 214–15; Egan, *Sand in a Whirlwind,* 246; Angel, *History of Nevada,* 151 (Numaga's prophecy).

18. Egan, *Sand in a Whirlwind*, 246–47; S. P. Davis, *History of Nevada*, 1:72; Angel, *History of Nevada*, 164.

19. Bancroft, *History*, 218–19; Angel, *History of Nevada*, 164. On the Mud Lake Massacre and the Black Rock War, see Sessions S. Wheeler, *The Nevada Desert*, 62–69; and Zanjani, *Sarah Winnemucca*, 77–79, 82–85.

20. Inter-Tribal Council of Nevada, *Numa*, 65–66; Zanjani, *Sarah Winnemucca*, 78–85, 259–60, chaps. 12–14; *TE*, May 19, 1860.

21. G. H. Smith, *History of the Comstock Lode*, 21–23, 27; *MD*, April 28, 1860; *TE*, May 19, 1860; Thompson, *Tennessee Letters*, 153. The Gold Hill miners, apparently anxious to return to normal practices, shortened the exemption period to twenty days on May 18 (*TE*, June 2, 1860).

22. Alfred Cumming, "Report," 15; *TE*, May 19, 1860.

23. *TE*, June 2, 1860; Robert W. Ellison, *Territorial Lawmen of Nevada*, 442–43, 448–50; Russell R. Elliott, *Servant of Power: A Political Biography of Senator William M. Stewart*, 16. On the tenure of territorial judges, see Kermit H. Hall, "Hacks and Derelicts Revisited: American Territorial Judiciary, 1789–1959," 276.

24. Angel, *History of Nevada*, 73; Thompson, *Tennessee Letters*, 158–59, 161.

25. Howard R. Lamar, *Dakota Territory, 1861–1889: A Study of Frontier Politics*, 56–58; Robert D. Ilisevich, *Galusha Grow: The People's Candidate*, 158–59, 163–65, 199. On Smith, see Guy L. Rocha, "How Nevada Became 'Nevada,'" 71–73.

26. Lamar, *Dakota Territory*, 17, 58–60; Ilisevich, *Galusha Grow*, 191–93; Browne, *Peep at Washoe*, 55.

---

10 · SUCH A MOTLEY CROWD: THE 1860 CENSUS

1. Ronald M. James, *The Roar and the Silence: A History of Virginia City and the Comstock Lode*, 37; Myron Angel, *History of Nevada*, 75; Alfred Cumming, "Report," 15–16; David Thompson, *The Tennessee Letters: From Carson Valley, 1857–1860*, 109–10; Stanley W. Paher, *Las Vegas: As It Began—As It Grew*, 32–33; "Esmeralda." Public letter, September 19, 1860. *MD*, September 29, 1860.

2. R. M. James, *Roar and Silence*, 54–57.

3. Ibid., 34–37.

4. J. Ross Browne, *A Peep at Washoe and Washoe Revisited*, 80, 82; Angel,

History of Nevada, 74; R. M. James, *Roar and Silence,* 25. Although Myron Angel states that no lawyers were practicing, lawyers' names *do* appear in the divorce records of the period.

5. Sally Zanjani, "Sam Brown: The Evolution of a Frontier Villain," 6–10; Angel, *History of Nevada,* 357. Peel did not arrive on the Comstock until two years after Brown's death.

6. Robert W. Ellison, *Territorial Lawmen of Nevada,* 245–46, 263, 270, 276–77, 476; Zanjani, "Sam Brown," 6–10. On men who worked on both sides of the line, see Sally Zanjani, *Goldfield: The Last Gold Rush on the Western Frontier,* 204.

7. R. W. Ellison, *Territorial Lawmen of Nevada,* 278; R. M. James, *Roar and Silence,* 31–32, 260–61; Malcolm J. Rohrbough, *Days of Gold: The California Gold Rush and the American Nation,* 94; Angel, *History of Nevada,* 75; Augustin Hale to mother, December 16, 1860; to mother et al., March 16, 1862, Augustin Hale Papers.

8. Browne, *Peep at Washoe,* 30. On Julia Bulette, see Susan James, "Julia Bulette's Boudoir."

9. I have primarily followed Eilley Orrum's statements in her Cowan divorce suit, which diverge somewhat from other sources on dates. The "piece of land" she received as alimony was probably the Washoe Valley site of Bowers mansion (see Probate Court Records, 52–57). See also Bancroft, *History of Nevada, 1540–1888,* 171n60; and Angel, *History of Nevada,* 39. Henry DeGroot notes that Sandy Bowers was Scotch, not Irish (*The Comstock Papers,* 44–45).

10. Kathryn Dunn Totton, "Hannah Keziah Clapp: The Life and Career of a Pioneer Nevada Educator, 1824–1908," 167–69, 173, 180–81.

11. Sarah Winnemucca Hopkins, *Life among the Piutes: Their Wrongs and Claims;* Sally Zanjani, *Sarah Winnemucca.*

12. Ronald M. James and Kenneth H. Fliess, "Women of the Mining West," 23–24. Nevada census database available at http://www.nevadaculture.org, as provided by Ronald James. Divorces are reported in the Probate Court Records, 27–30, 44–45, 50–65, 72–73, 83–84, 86–89. On Utah law, see Carol C. Madsen, "'At Their Peril': Utah Law and the Case of Plural Wives, 1850–1900," 430–33.

13. Probate Court Records; Thompson, *Tennessee Letters,* 146; Glenda Riley, *Divorce: An American Tradition,* 124; Browne, *Peep at Washoe,* 92–93.

14. Probate Court Records; H. Hamlin, ed., *Knott Reminiscences,* 22.

15. Nancy J. Taniguchi, "Weaving a Different World: Women and the Cali-

fornia Gold Rush," 144; *TE*, June 9, 1860; Grant H. Smith, *The History of the Comstock Lode*, 30–31. On western divorce and new beginnings, see Riley, *Divorce: An American Tradition*, 5–6.

16. Polly Aird, "Escape from Zion: The United States Army Escort of Mormon Apostates, 1859," 210–11; Thompson, *Tennessee Letters*, 156.

17. Sally Zanjani, *The Unspiked Rail: Memoir of a Nevada Rebel*, 8, 25; Fred Dressler, oral history, April 10, 1984, 1–6.

18. N. A. Hummel, *General History and Resources of Washoe County, Nevada*, 13.

19. Jane Brown to mother, March 17, 1861; Joshua Brown to father, March 16, 1861; *Nevada State Journal*, September 10, 1878, Peleg Brown Papers. See also Benjamin Damonte Papers.

---

11 · Territory! 1861

1. David Thompson, *The Tennessee Letters: From Carson Valley, 1857–1860*, 177–79.

2. David Morris Potter, *Lincoln and His Party in the Secession Crisis*, esp. 9–19, 45, 81, 88, 112, 135–36, 249–50, 234–38, 278–79; Howard R. Lamar, *Dakota Territory, 1861–1889: A Study of Frontier Politics*, 60–61; Howard R. Lamar, *The Far Southwest: A Territorial History*, 9.

3. Lamar, *Dakota Territory*, 60–63.

4. Ibid., 17, 60–65; Potter, *Lincoln and His Party*, 277–78. On popular sovereignty, see esp. Lamar, *Dakota Territory*, 62–65; and David Morris Potter, *The Impending Crisis, 1848–1861*, 328–29.

5. Michael W. Bowers, *The Sagebrush State: Nevada's History, Government, and Politics*, 13–14; Robert D. Ilisevich, *Galusha Grow: The People's Candidate*, 178–79; Russell R. Elliott, *History of Nevada*, 68.

6. Elliott, *History of Nevada*, 74–75; John Koontz, *Political History of Nevada, 1965*, 21, 30; Stanley W. Paher, *Nevada Ghost Towns and Mining Camps*, 466; Grant H. Smith, *History of the Comstock Lode*, 25; Eugene P. Moehring, *Urbanism and Empire in the Far West, 1840–1890*, 143, 166. However, a large swath of territory known as the "Unexplored Desert" from roughly south of Belmont to the California border remained scarcely populated and little known (Sally Zanjani, *Jack Longstreet*, 48–50).

7. Sam P. Davis, ed., *History of Nevada*, 1:268–69; Lamar, *Dakota Territory*, 60; Hubert Howe Bancroft, *History of Nevada, 1540–1888*, 92.

8. Augustin Hale to mother, February 24, 1861, Augustin Hale Papers (this item is reproduced by permission of *The Huntington Library, San Marino, California*); W. H. Watford, "Confederate Western Ambitions," 161, 166–67, 174–75, 186–87.

9. S. P. Davis, *History of Nevada*, 1:270–71; Sally Zanjani, "Sam Brown: The Evolution of a Frontier Villain," 7–8; A. Russell Buchanan, *David S. Terry of California*, 123.

10. Myron Angel, *History of Nevada*, 266; *Silver Age*, August 26, 1861; Hale to mother et al., July 7, 1861, Hale Papers.

11. Watford, "Confederate Western Ambitions," 182–86; Angel, *History of Nevada*, 264–65.

12. I. P. Corrigan to Alsop and Company, Adolph Sutro Papers; Buchanan, *David S. Terry*, 113, 120–23, 129, 131; Arthur Quinn, *The Rivals: William Gwin, David Broderick, and the Birth of California*, 169.

13. Buchanan, *David S. Terry*, 113, 120–23, 129. William Stewart harbored some Southern leanings but, sensing the direction of the political wind, entered the U.S. Senate as a Lincoln Republican in 1865 (Russell R. Elliott, *Servant of Power: A Political Biography of Senator William M. Stewart*, 279n61).

14. "Dr. Selden A. McMeans, Nevada's Early Politician Doctor"; Jane McMeans, telephone interview with author, May 11, 2004; Angel, *History of Nevada*, 266. On the Knights of the Golden Circle, see Potter, *Lincoln and His Party*, 221–22; and Potter, *Impending Crisis*, 197.

15. Patrick Henry Clayton, file, Russell W. McDonald Papers; Angel, *History of Nevada*, 265.

16. George R. Brown, ed., *Reminiscences of Senator William M. Stewart of Nevada*, 137–39; Effie Mona Mack, *Nevada*, 188; Buchanan, *David S. Terry*, 121–22; Angel, *History of Nevada*, 265.

17. The votes on the constitution, and especially the secessionist influence, are discussed in Bancroft, *History*, 178–83; Elliott, *History of Nevada*, 81–89; Elliott, *Servant of Power*, 33, 41–42; David A. Johnson, *Founding the Far West: California, Oregon, and Nevada, 1840–1890*, esp. 212–13; Angel, *History of Nevada*, 84; and Don W. Driggs and Leonard E. Goodall, *Nevada Politics and Government*, 36–38. On later developments, see Sally Zanjani, "A Theory of Critical Realignment: The Nevada Example, 1892–1908," 259–80.

18. Michael J. Brodhead, "The Nevada Constitution's Paramount Allegiance Clause."

19. Of the thirty-five delegates at the first constitutional convention, thirty-three were former Californians (Johnson, *Founding the Far West*, 191).

EPILOGUE · GHOSTS WHO WALK

1. David Thompson, *The Tennessee Letters: From Carson Valley, 1857–1860*, 110.

2. Myron Angel, *History of Nevada*, 40–41.

3. Phillip I. Earl, "'Lucky Bill' Got Lucky Again . . . or Did He?"

4. See Sally Zanjani, "Sam Brown: The Evolution of a Frontier Villain."

5. *Reno Gazette-Journal*, June 18, 2001, 1B.

6. *Reno Gazette-Journal*, March 7, 2002, 1C, 7C.

7. Henry DeGroot, *The Comstock Papers*, 30–31; Charles H. Shinn, *The Story of the Mine*, 46; Eliot Lord, *Comstock Mining and Miners*, 411–13.

BIBLIOGRAPHY

NEWSPAPERS

Alta California (San Francisco)
Mountain Democrat (Placerville, CA)
Record Courier (Gardinerville, NV)
Sacramento Bee
Sacramento Union
San Francisco Bulletin
San Francisco Herald
Silver Age (Carson City, NV)
Territorial Enterprise (Genoa and later Carson City, Utah Territory; subsequently Virginia City, Nevada Territory and state)

OTHER SOURCES

Aird, Polly. "Escape from Zion: The United States Army Escort of Mormon Apostates, 1859." *Nevada Historical Society Quarterly* 44 (Fall 2001): 196–237.

Angel, Myron. *History of Nevada.* Oakland: Thompson and West, 1881.

Arrington, Leonard J. *Brigham Young: American Moses.* New York: Alfred A. Knopf, 1985.

———. *Great Basin Kingdom.* Cambridge, MA: Harvard University Press, 1958.

———. *The Mormons in Nevada.* Las Vegas: Las Vegas Sun, 1979.

Arrington, Leonard J., and Davis Bitton. *The Mormon Experience: A History of the Latter-Day Saints.* New York: Alfred A. Knopf, 1979.

Bagley, Will. *Blood of the Prophets: Brigham Young and the Massacre at Mountain Meadows.* Norman: University of Oklahoma Press, 2002.

Bibliography

————, ed. *Frontiersman: Abner Blackburn's Narrative*. University of Utah Press, 1992.

Bancroft, Hubert Howe. *History of Nevada*. Reno: University of Nevada Press, 1981.

Bayer, Chris W. *Profit, Plots and Lynching*. Self-published, 1995.

Bowers, Michael W. *The Sagebrush State: Nevada's History, Government, and Politics*. Reno: University of Nevada Press, 1996.

Brodhead, Michael J. "The Nevada Constitution's Paramount Allegiance Clause." In *Uncovering Nevada's Past: A Primary Source History of the Silver State*, edited by John B. Reid and Ronald M. James, 31–32. Reno: University of Nevada Press, 2004.

Brooks, Juanita. "The Mormons in Carson County, Utah Territory." *Nevada Historical Society Quarterly* 8 (Spring 1965): 4–23.

————. *The Mountain Meadows Massacre*. Stanford, CA: Stanford University Press, 1950.

Brown, George R., ed. *Reminiscences of Senator William M. Stewart of Nevada*. New York: Neale, 1908.

Brown, J. R. "Poker." "Testimony." In *Joseph Jones v. John Q. Adams*, appeal to the Nevada Supreme Court, 1881, Nevada Archives and Records, Carson City, 158–70.

Brown, Peleg. Papers. Nevada Historical Society, Reno.

Brown, Richard Maxwell. *No Duty to Retreat: Violence and Values in American History and Society*. New York: Oxford University Press, 1991.

Browne, J. Ross. *A Peep at Washoe and Washoe Revisited*. 1860 and 1863. Reprint, Balboa Island, CA: Paisano Press, 1959.

Buchanan, A. Russell. *David S. Terry of California*. San Marino, CA: Huntington Library, 1956.

Burrows, William E. *Vigilante!* New York: Harcourt Brace Jovanovich, 1976.

Butler, James T. *Isaac Roop: Pioneer and Political Leader of Northeastern California*. Janesville, CA: Lassen County Historical Society, 1994.

Cappon, Lester J. *Virginia Newspapers, 1821–1935*. New York: D. Appleton-Century, n.d.

Carlson, Helen S. *Nevada Place Names: A Geographical Dictionary*. Reno: University of Nevada Press, 1974.

Carter, Kate B. *The Mormons in Nevada*. Salt Lake City: Daughters of the Utah Pioneers, 1946.

Chalfant, Willie A. *The Story of Inyo*. Bishop, CA: Chalfant Press, 1933.

Bibliography

Cheel, Chester W. "Historic Development of Western Utah between 118 and 120 Degrees West Longitude, 1827–1861." Typescript, University of Nevada, Reno, 1939.

Cipriani, Leonetto. *California and Overland Diaries.* Translated and edited by Ernest Falbo. Portland, OR: Champoeg Press, 1962.

Clayton, Patrick H. File, Russell W. McDonald Papers. Nevada Historical Society, Reno.

Comstock, Henry T. P. *Chronology of the Comstock Lode.* Reno: Nevada Historical Society, n.d.

Crane, James M. *The Past, the Present and the Future of the Pacific.* San Francisco: Sterett, 1856.

Cumming, Alfred. "Report." February 1, 1860. File microcopies of records in the National Archives, no. 12, State Department Territorial Papers, Utah Series, vol. 2, January 5, 1860–January 3, 1863. Special Collections and Archives, Merrill Library, Utah State University, Logan. Utah Reel 569.

Damonte, Benjamin. Papers. Private collection.

Dangberg, Grace. *Washo Tales Translated with an Introduction.* Privately printed, 1968.

Davis, Ryan. "Charles Daggett: Nevada's First Doctor." *Greasewood Tablettes* 14 (Fall 2003): 1–2.

Davis, Sam P., ed. *History of Nevada.* Vols. 1–2. Reno: Elms, 1913.

———. "Ormsby County." In *History of Nevada,* edited by Sam P. Davis, 2:973–96. Reno: Elms, 1913.

DeGroot, Henry. *The Comstock Papers.* 1876. Reprint, Reno: Grace Dangberg Foundation, 1985.

De Quille, Dan [William Wright]. *The Big Bonanza.* 1876. Reprint, New York: Alfred A. Knopf, 1947.

DeVoto, Bernard. *The Year of Decision, 1846.* Boston: Houghton Mifflin, 1942.

Downs, James. "Differential Response to White Contact." In *The Washo Indians of California and Nevada,* edited by Warren L. d'Azevedo, 115–37. University of Utah Anthropological Papers 67. Salt Lake City: University of Utah Press, 1963.

———. *The Two Worlds of the Washo: An Indian Tribe of California and Nevada.* New York: Holt, Rinehart, and Winston, 1966.

"Dr. Selden A. McMeans, Nevada's Early Politician Doctor." *Greasewood Tablettes* 15 (Spring 2004): 1–2.

Dressler, Fred. Oral History, April 10, 1984. Oral History Program, University of Nevada, Reno.

Driggs, Don W., and Goodall, Leonard E. *Nevada Politics and Government.* Lincoln: University of Nebraska Press, 1996.

Eakin, Emily. "Reopening a Mormon Murder Mystery." *New York Times,* October 12, 2002, A19, 21.

Earl, Phillip I. "'Lucky Bill' Got Lucky Again . . . or Did He?" *Nevada Appeal,* May 16, 1982, n.p.

Eblen, Jack E. *The First and Second United States Empires: Governors and Territorial Government, 1784–1912.* Pittsburgh: University of Pittsburgh Press, 1968.

Egan, Ferol. *Sand in a Whirlwind: The Paiute Indian War of 1860.* New York: Doubleday, 1972.

Elliott, Russell R. *History of Nevada.* Lincoln: University of Nebraska Press, 1973.

———. *Servant of Power: A Political Biography of Senator William M. Stewart.* Reno: University of Nevada Press, 1983.

Ellison, Joseph. "Designs for a Pacific Republic." *Oregon Historical Quarterly* 31 (December 1930): 319–42.

Ellison, Robert W. *First Impressions: The Trail through Carson Valley, 1848–1852.* Minden, NV: Hot Springs Mountain Press, 2001.

———. *Territorial Lawmen of Nevada.* Vol. 1. Minden, NV: Hot Springs Mountain Press, 1999.

"Esmeralda." Public letter, September 19, 1860. *Mountain Democrat,* September 29, 1860.

Fairfield, Asa M. *A Pioneer History of Lassen County.* San Francisco: Crocker, 1916.

Ficken, Robert E. "The Fraser River Humbug: Americans and Gold in the British Pacific Northwest." *Western Historical Quarterly* 33 (Autumn 2002): 297–313.

Francaviglia, Richard V. "Maps and Mining: Some Historical Examples from the Great Basin." *Mining History Journal* (2001): 66–82.

Frazer, Robert W. *Forts of the West.* Norman: University of Oklahoma Press, 1965.

Furniss, Norman F. *The Mormon Conflict, 1850–1859.* New Haven, CT: Yale University Press, 1960.

Bibliography

Gilbert, Bil. *Westering Man: The Life of Joseph Walker.* New York: Atheneum, 1983.

Gordon, Mary McDougall, ed. *Overland to California with the Pioneer Line: The Gold Rush Diary of Bernard J. Reid.* Stanford, CA: Stanford University Press, 1983.

Griffith, Martin. "What's Nevada's Oldest Town?" *Nevada Magazine* (September–October 1998): 10–15, 77.

Grosh, Ethan Allen, and Hosea Ballou. Papers. 1849–1857. Nevada Historical Society, Reno.

Hale, Augustin. Papers. 1799–1904. Henry E. Huntington Library, San Marino, CA.

Hall, Kermit H. "Hacks and Derelicts Revisited: American Territorial Judiciary, 1789–1959." *Western Historical Quarterly* 12 (July 1981): 273–87.

Hamlin, H., ed. *Knott Reminiscences.* Placerville, CA: Pioneer Press, 1947.

Harte, Bret. *Tales of the Gold Rush.* New York: Heritage Press, 1944.

Hazlett, Fanny G., and Gertrude H. Randall. "Historical Sketch and Reminiscences of Dayton, Nevada." *Nevada Historical Society Papers, 1921-1922* 3 (1922): 3–93.

Hill, Edward E. *The Office of Indian Affairs, 1824–1880: Historical Sketches.* New York: Clearwater, 1974.

Holmes, Kenneth L., ed. *Covered Wagon Women: Diaries and Letters from the Western Trails.* Vols. 4, 7. Lincoln: University of Nebraska Press, 1985–1987.

Hopkins, Sarah Winnemucca. *Life among the Piutes: Their Wrongs and Claims.* 1883. Reprint, Bishop, CA: Sierra Media, 1969.

Hull, Dorothy. "The Movement in Oregon for the Establishment of a Pacific Coast Republic." *Quarterly of the Oregon Historical Society* 17 (September 1916): 177–200.

Hummel, N. A. *General History and Resources of Washoe County, Nevada.* N.p.: Nevada Educational Association, 1888.

Hunt, Rockwell D. *John Bidwell: Prince of California Pioneers.* Caldwell, ID: Caxton Printers, 1942.

Hutcheson, Austin E. "Before the Comstock: Memoirs of William Hickman Dolman." *New Mexico Historical Review* 22 (July 1947): 205–46.

———. "A Life of Fifty Years in Nevada: The Memoirs of Penrod of the Comstock Lode, Commentary, Notes, and Transcription by Austin E. Hutcheson." *Nevada Historical Society Quarterly* 1 (Winter 1958): 132–39.

Bibliography

Hyde, John, Jun. *Mormonism: Its Leaders and Designs*. New York: W. P. Fetridge, 1857.

Hyde, Myrtle S. *Orson Hyde: The Olive Branch of Israel*. Salt Lake City: Agreka Books, 2000.

Ilisevich, Robert D. *Galusha Grow: The People's Candidate*. Pittsburgh: University of Pittsburgh Press, 1988.

Inter-Tribal Council of Nevada. *Numa: A Northern Paiute History*. Salt Lake City: University of Utah Printing Service, 1976.

———. *Wa She Shu: A Washo Tribal History*. Salt Lake City: University of Utah Printing Service, 1976.

James, Ronald M. *The Roar and the Silence: A History of Virginia City and the Comstock Lode*. Reno: University of Nevada Press, 1998.

James, Ronald M., and Kenneth H. Fliess. "Women of the Mining West." In *Comstock Women: The Making of a Mining Community*, edited by Ronald M. James and C. Elizabeth Raymond, 17–42. Reno: University of Nevada Press, 1998.

James, Susan. "Julia Bulette's Boudoir." *Nevada Magazine* 64 (March–April 2004): 22–23.

Johnson, David A. *Founding the Far West: California, Oregon, and Nevada, 1840–1890*. Berkeley and Los Angeles: University of California Press, 1992.

Jones, Beatrice F. "Hanging of Lucky Bill." Special Collections, University of Nevada, Reno.

Josephy, Alvin M. *The Indian Heritage of America*. New York: Bantam, 1969.

Kennedy, Elijah R. *The Contest for California in 1861*. Boston: Houghton Mifflin, 1912.

Koontz, John. *Political History of Nevada, 1965*. 5th ed. Carson City, NV: State Printing Office, 1965.

Kowalewski, Michael. "Romancing the Gold Rush: The Literature of the California Frontier." In *Rooted in Barbarous Soil: People, Culture and Community in Gold Rush California*, edited by Kevin Starr and Richard J. Orsi, 204–25. Berkeley and Los Angeles: University of California Press, 2000.

Kroeber, A. L. *Handbook of the Indians of California*. Bureau of American Ethnology Bulletin 78. Washington, DC: GPO, 1925.

Lamar, Howard R. *Dakota Territory, 1861–1889: A Study of Frontier Politics*. New Haven, CT: Yale University Press, 1956.

———. *The Far Southwest: A Territorial History*. Rev. ed. Albuquerque: University of New Mexico Press, 2000.

Bibliography

Lingenfelter, Richard E., and Gash, Karen R. *The Newspapers of Nevada: A History and Bibliography, 1854–1979.* Reno: University of Nevada Press, 1984.

Lord, Eliot. *Comstock Mining and Miners.* 1883. Reprint, Berkeley: Howell-North, 1959.

Mack, Effie Mona. *Nevada.* Glendale, CA: Arthur H. Clark, 1936.

Madsen, Brigham D. *The Bannock of Idaho.* Caldwell, ID: Caxton Printers, 1983. Reprint, Moscow, ID: University of Idaho Press, 1996.

Madsen, Carol C. "'At Their Peril': Utah Law and the Case of Plural Wives, 1850–1900." *Western Historical Quarterly* 21 (November 1990): 425–43.

Makley, Michael J. *The Hanging of Lucky Bill.* Woodfords, CA: Eastern Sierra Press, 1993.

McDermott, John D. *A Guide to the Indian Wars of the West.* Lincoln: University of Nebraska Press, 1998.

McPherson, James M. *Battle Cry of Freedom: The Civil War Era.* New York: Oxford University Press, 1988.

Merk, Frederick. *Manifest Destiny and Mission in American History: A Reinterpretation.* New York: Alfred A. Knopf, 1963.

Miller, William C. "The Pyramid Lake Indian War of 1860." Pts. 1 and 2. *Nevada Historical Society Quarterly* 1 (Summer 1957): 37–53; (Fall 1957): 100–113.

Moehring, Eugene P. *Urbanism and Empire in the Far West, 1840–1890.* Reno: University of Nevada Press, 2004.

Morgan, Dale L. *The Humboldt: Highroad of the West.* New York: Farrar and Rinehart, 1943.

———. "The State of Deseret." *Utah Historical Quarterly* 8 (April–October 1940): 64–251.

Nevada Historical Society Papers, 1913–1916. Vol. 1. Carson City: State Printing Office, 1917.

Nickerson, Benjamin R. *A Statement of the Grounds of the Claim of the Grosch Consolidated Gold and Silver Mining Company, to the Comstock Mine in Nevada Territory: Together with Their Reply to the Attacks of the Press.* San Francisco: Towne and Bacon, 1863. Copy in the Rare Book Collection at the Henry E. Huntington Library, San Marino, CA.

Owens, Kenneth N. *History.* Vol. 2 of *Archeological and Historical Investigation of the Mormon-Carson Emigrant Trail: Eldorado and Toiyabe National Forests.* Placerville, CA: U.S. Forest Service, 1990.

————. "Government and Politics in the Nineteenth-Century West." In *Historians and the American West,* edited by Michael P. Malone, 148–76. Lincoln: University of Nebraska Press, 1983.

Page, Albert R. "Orson Hyde and the Carson Valley Mission, 1855–1857." Master's thesis, Brigham Young University, 1970.

Paher, Stanley W., ed. *Emigrant Shadows.* Virginia City, NV: Western Trails Research Association, 2002.

————. "From Emigrant Trading Posts to Nevada Towns: Genoa and Dayton—but Which Was First?" *Overland Journal* 21 (Winter 2003–2004): 138–53.

————. *Las Vegas: As It Began—As It Grew.* Las Vegas: Nevada Publications, 1971.

————. *Nevada Ghost Towns and Mining Camps.* Berkeley, CA: Howell-North, 1970.

Parker, Captain. "Testimony." In *Joseph Jones v. John Q. Adams,* appeal to the Nevada Supreme Court, 1881, Nevada Archives and Records, Carson City, 170–75.

Patterson, Edna B., Louise A. Ulph, and Victor Goodwin. *Nevada's Northeast Frontier.* Reno: University of Nevada Press, 1969.

Paul, Rodman W. *California Gold: The Beginning of Mining in the Far West.* Lincoln: University of Nebraska Press, 1947.

Pomeroy, Earl. *The Pacific Slope: A History of California, Oregon, Washington, Idaho, Utah, and Nevada.* New York: Alfred A. Knopf, 1968.

Potter, David Morris. *The Impending Crisis, 1848–1861.* New York: Harper and Rowe, 1976.

————. *Lincoln and His Party in the Secession Crisis.* New Haven, CT: Yale University Press, 1942.

————, ed. *Trail to California: The Overland Journal of Vincent Geiger and Wakeman Bryarly.* New Haven, CT: Yale University Press, 1945.

Price, John A. "Some Aspects of the Washo Life Cycle." In *The Washo Indians of California and Nevada,* edited by Warren L. d'Azevedo, 96–114. Anthropological Papers 67. Salt Lake City: University of Utah Press, 1963.

————. "Washo Prehistory: A Review of Research." In *The Washo Indians of California and Nevada,* edited by Warren L. d'Azevedo, 78–95. Anthropological Papers 67. Salt Lake City: University of Utah Press, 1963.

Probate Court Records. Carson County, Utah Territory, October 1855–July 30, 1861. Nevada State Library and Archives, Carson City.

Bibliography

Quinn, Arthur. *The Rivals: William Gwin, David Broderick, and the Birth of California.* Lincoln: University of Nebraska Press, 1994.

Rasmussen, Louis J. *San Francisco Ship Passenger Lists.* Vol. 1. Colma, CA: San Francisco Historic Record and Genealogy Bulletin, 1965.

Ratay, Myra S. *Pioneers of the Ponderosa.* Privately printed, 1973.

Richards, Kent D. "Washoe Territory: Rudimentary Government in Nevada." *Arizona and the West* 11 (Autumn 1969): 213–32.

Riley, Glenda. *Divorce: An American Tradition.* New York: Oxford University Press, 1991.

Rocha, Guy L. "How Nevada Became 'Nevada,'" *Nevada Magazine* 56 (April 1996): 70–75.

Rohrbough, Malcolm J. *Days of Gold: The California Gold Rush and the American Nation.* Berkeley and Los Angeles: University of California Press, 1997.

Royce, Sarah. *A Frontier Lady: Recollections of the Gold Rush and Early California.* 1932. Reprint, Lincoln: University of Nebraska Press, 1977.

Rusco, Elmer R. *"Good Time Coming?" Black Nevadans in the Nineteenth Century.* Westport, CT: Greenwood Press, 1975.

———. Unpublished manuscript. Author's collection.

Sandos, James A. "'Because He Is a Liar and a Thief': Conquering the Residents of 'Old' California, 1850–1880." In *Rooted in Barbarous Soil: People, Culture and Community in Gold Rush California,* edited by Kevin Starr and Richard J. Orsi, 86–112. Berkeley and Los Angeles: University of California Press, 2000.

Schoeck, Helmut. *Envy: A Theory of Social Behavior.* Indianapolis: Liberty Fund, 1969.

Scrugham, James G. *Nevada.* 3 vols. Chicago: American Historical Society, 1935.

Shinn, Charles H. *The Story of the Mine.* 1896. Reprint, Reno: University of Nevada Press, 1980.

Smith, Grant H. *The History of the Comstock Lode.* Geology and Mining Series no. 37. Reno: Nevada State Bureau of Mines and the Mackay School of Mines, 1943.

Smith, Henry Nash, ed. *Mark Twain of the "Enterprise."* Berkeley and Los Angeles: University of California Press, 1957.

Spence, Mary Lee, and Donald Jackson, eds. *The Expeditions of John Charles Fremont.* 2 vols. Urbana: University of Illinois Press, 1973.

Bibliography

Stenhouse, T. B. H. *The Rocky Mountain Saints: A Full and Complete History of the Mormons, from the First Vision of Joseph Smith to the Last Courtship of Brigham Young.* New York: D. Appleton, 1873.

Stewart, George R. *The California Trail.* American Trails Series. New York: McGraw-Hill, 1962.

———. *Committee of Vigilance.* Boston: Houghton Mifflin, 1964.

Sutro, Adolph. Papers. 1853–1931. Henry E. Huntington Library, San Marino, CA.

Taniguchi, Nancy J. "Weaving a Different World: Women and the California Gold Rush." In *Rooted in Barbarous Soil: People, Culture and Community in Gold Rush California,* edited by Kevin Starr and Richard J. Orsi, 141–68. Berkeley and Los Angeles: University of California Press, 2000.

Thompson, David. *The Tennessee Letters: From Carson Valley, 1857–1860.* Reno: Grace Dangberg Foundation, 1983.

Totton, Kathryn Dunn. "Hannah Keziah Clapp: The Life and Career of a Pioneer Nevada Educator, 1824–1908." *Nevada Historical Society Quarterly* 20 (Fall 1977): 167–83.

Townley, John M. "Stalking Horse for the Pony Express: The Chorpenning Mail Contracts between California and Utah, 1851–1860." *Arizona and the West* 24 (Autumn 1982): 229–52.

———. *Tough Little Town on the Truckee, 1868–1900.* Reno: Great Basin Studies Center, 1983.

Trimmer, Arnold R. "Reminiscences of the Number One Ranch in Carson Valley, Nevada." 1982. Oral History Program, University of Nevada, Reno.

U.S. Department of the Interior. *Report, 1868–1869.* 40th Cong., 3d sess. Washington, DC: GPO, 1869.

Utley, Robert M. *Frontiersmen in Blue: The United States Army and the Indian, 1848–1865.* Lincoln: University of Nebraska Press, 1967.

Vaught, David. "After the Gold Rush: Replicating the Rural Midwest in the Sacramento Valley." *Western Historical Quarterly* 34 (Winter 2003): 446–67.

Watford, W. H. "Confederate Western Ambitions." *Southwestern Historical Quarterly* 44 (October 1940): 161–87.

West, Don. "Troubled Days in Carson Valley." In *Nevada Official Bicentennial Book,* edited by Stanley W. Paher, 54–55. Las Vegas: Nevada Publications, 1976.

Bibliography

Wheeler, Sessions S. *The Nevada Desert*. Caldwell, ID: Caxton Printers, 1972.

White, Richard. *It's Your Misfortune and None of My Own: A New History of the American West*. Norman: University of Oklahoma Press, 1991.

Williamson, Lynn E. "From Our Library Collection." *Nevada Historical Society Quarterly* 16 (Spring 1973): 24–25.

Zanjani, Sally. *Goldfield: The Last Gold Rush on the Western Frontier*. Athens: Ohio University Press, 1992.

———. *Jack Longstreet*. Las Vegas: Nevada Publications, 1988.

———. "Sam Brown: The Evolution of a Frontier Villain." *Pacific Historian* 29 (Winter 1985): 4–17.

———. *Sarah Winnemucca*. Lincoln: University of Nebraska Press, 2001.

———. "A Theory of Critical Realignment: The Nevada Example, 1892–1908." *Pacific Historical Review* 48 (May 1979): 259–80.

———. *The Unspiked Rail: Memoir of a Nevada Rebel*. Reno: University of Nevada Press, 1981.

INTERVIEWS

Harmon, Barbara, telephone interview with author, April 4, 2003.

Hunter, Lillis, telephone interview with author, August 8, 2001, May 6, 2003.

McMeans, Jane, telephone interview with author, May 11, 2003.

Olds, Leonard, telephone interview with author, July 31, 2003.

Wegman, Charles T., telephone interview with author, March 6, 2002.

INDEX

Index

Index